$6.95

DARRINGTON

Mining Town/Timber Town

By Elizabeth S. Poehlman

The line drawing on the cover was created by Darrington artist Peter K. Selvig and is based on an early photo. The chapter logo by Peter K. Selvig shows the miner's pick and the logger's axe, symbolizing the two major influences on Darrington's development.

To Darrington, with Love

Foreword

Darrington is as much a memory as it is a community. Tucked away deep in the Cascade Mountains of Washington, it has held an aloof isolation from the rest of the country. Its ways, its philosophy, its economy have never quite left the world of old America where a community was alone and independent, part of the larger community of nation but still a separate, individual entity, making its own living, its own values, its own fun in its own way.

But even Darrington is leaving its past. Modern gadgets are bringing the world to the little community. Time is thinning the ranks of old timers who knew the town when it was aborning.

Beginning with the Indian groups that were there first, Elizabeth Poehlman paints prose pictures of the people, the valley, the mountains and forests as they were in the past and are now. They are fascinating pictures, woven together by someone who loves them all to make a tapestry of the past — Darrington's and America's. Here is a story that should be treasured by everyone in and out of the little town in the hills.

Allan May
Staff Writer, *The Everett Herald*
Everett, Washington

Table of Contents

Photographs

Preface

"You're writing a book about Darrington?" people have asked me incredulously. "What's there to write about in a little place like that?" My answer has been: "Plenty." In fact, in the pages to follow I have only begun to touch on Darrington's story, roughly covering the years prior to white settlement through 1950.

I have learned that *every place*, no matter how small, has a history, and that *every person* has a history, too. In fact, every place has many histories, composed of the individual stories of the people who have populated it. Darrington has a fascinating history composed by colorful, interesting people.

I have also learned that even Darrington, isolated as it was from other places and other people in its early years, presents a micro-history of the United States. Exploration, settlement, exploitation of resources, labor unrest, railroads and roads, the Depression — all of the headings I have seen in my history textbooks became real as I learned about life in this little settlement up in the northeast corner of Snohomish County, Washington.

The exciting part of researching the community's history is that in Darrington the past is so recent. I come from the east coast where the beginnings of white man's history, at least, are rooted in the seventeenth and eighteenth centuries. Darrington's history as a community began at the very end of the nineteenth century. I found myself in the enviable position of piecing together the area's story by talking with some of the people who were here when it all was beginning.

8

The process of putting Darrington's history into written order was often frustrated by the divergent stories of the past that people told to me. I soon realized that it is virtually impossible to write a *complete* history. To be complete, a narrative of Darrington — as of any place — would have to recount the personal stories of every individual who ever lived there; for each person saw, experienced and made this town's past and present and influenced its future in an individual way.

When I acknowledged the impossibility of writing a complete history, I settled down to the more workable task of putting into order some of the major events of the past years. In addition I sought to paint a word picture of the town as it emerged and to recount the individual stories of some of the townspeople whose lives reflected or shaped the time and place in which they lived. I am aware of the fact that many readers will know of other individuals with whom I could have talked to gain another point of view, but I had to stop somewhere.

One of the joys of researching and writing this book over a period of seven and a half years has been meeting and talking with many people in Darrington and elsewhere who could help me put together the story of the town. The helpfulness of these people and their encouragement kept me going when the whole research-writing process grew difficult and discouraging.

In addition to the people mentioned in the text, photo credits and chapter notes there are a number of others whose help I want to acknowledge: Jerry Zubrod, manager of Washington Newspaper Publishers' Association, who helped me track down information on Darrington's newspapers; Kim Forman, regional public relations manager for Burlington Northern; Frank Perrin, public relations director for Burlington Northern; and L.M. Jenner, senior real estate representative for the railroad, all of whom worked on locating information about D. C. Linsley's railroad survey; Mrs. Maxine Hansen and Mrs. Joyce Aiken, of the Darrington District Ranger Station, Mt. Baker-Snoqualmie National Forest, for their assistance with historic Forest Service materials; U.S. Bureau of the Census for population figures; U.S. General Services Administration for names of postmasters and dates of service; the Darrington Post Office for use of documents showing the application for original postal service; Clifford B. Ellis of the Ellis Post Card Co., Arlington Washington, for his excellent reproductions of historical photographs; Mrs. Karyl Winn, curator of manuscripts,

University of Washington Library, and her staff; Mrs. Georgia Kloostra, supervisor, newspaper-microcopy section, University of Washington Library, and her staff; Allan May, my editor when I was correspondent for *The Everett Herald* and one of the early supporters of the book idea; Alice Elinor Lambert, who, despite her seniority, accepted me as a fellow-writer; Elden Abbott, Darrington pharmacist, who urged me to complete my book after I had abondoned it for a short time; Mrs. Jean Fournier Morgan, chairman of the board of Valley Publishing Co., Kent, who read and critiqued my incomplete manuscript; Dr. Robert E. Burke, editor of *The Pacific Northwest Quarterly,* who read my final rough draft; and advanced typing students at Kent-Meridian High School who typed the final manuscript.

I want to say special thanks to Elizabeth Goodall, my aunt and a retired history teacher, who encouraged me in special ways; to my husband, Paul, who only occasionally despaired of my finishing my project; to my sons, Kyle and Andy, who have grown up with the fact that "Mom is writing a book"; to other family members and friends who wouldn't let me quit; and to an exceptional group of babysitters in Darrington and Kent who made it possible for me to work on a book despite two small children.

Elizabeth S. Poehlman
Kent, Washington

Chapter 1

Up the Road To Darrington

The first trip up the Arlington-Darrington road is a long one. It takes about a year for the journey to shorten to the thirty miles it actually is. For the newcomer the thirty miles are a long trip to nowhere.

That's how we felt the first time we drove the road. The year was 1966. Then the route boasted more potholes than it does now and fewer miles of new asphalt and proper grading.

Paul drove the car that first trip. I held the map. The line from Arlington to Darrington did not look very long. It meandered along the North Fork of the Stillaguamish River in an inviting way. It went through only a few named places on its way east toward the Cascade mountains and Darrington.

Oso is one of the "towns" on the Arlington-Darrington road. We came on it suddenly around a curve. There was an abandoned school, a narrow, hump-backed bridge over Deer Creek, a small assortment of houses, a fire hall, two service

Darrington in 1926 looked small against the landscape of the Sauk and Stillaguamish Valleys. Today even fewer buildings can be seen from this same viewpoint on Gold Hill because of the tall second growth trees that have reforested the townsite and its surroundings. Photo by Darius Kinsey. Courtesy of Tom Ashe.

stations, one of which did double duty as a general store-post office. Then Oso was gone, and around another bend were scattered farms and more winding road.

On the map there was a place called Hazel. We would have missed it if we had not been driving slowly. A small black and white sign pointed out that this wide place in the road was Hazel. Other than that Hazel amounted to a pond and a couple of houses.

We drove another six miles, then crossed the narrow bridge over Squire Creek and climbed what is known as Sand Hill. The road lay beside heavy second growth of fir on one side. On the other side high-tension wires of Seattle City Light followed the road for a while. We passed a cemetery and a church, and there was Darrington, population 1,125, a state sign said. An old sign pointed the way to "city center." The route to city center zigzagged through town on a thin layer of asphalt.

So this was Darrington. Kind of shabby. Very small. Very dreary under an almost-going-to-rain sky. "City center" consisted of one street, paved and with sidewalks, a combination of characteristics which set it apart from every other street in town. There were two grocery stores, a hardware store, drug store, variety store, post office and bank, small clothing store, barber shop, two taverns, three gas stations, a small bowling alley, a real estate office, and a restaurant of sorts. At the east end of the main street was Gold Hill, rising like a giant roadblock.

Paul and I are city people. We had come to Darrington from Los Angeles and before that from suburban Philadelphia, Pa. I guess we suffered a little cultural shock that first day in Darrington. We had a week to make up our minds whether we would make it our home.

We decided to stay. We stayed for nearly seven years. In those seven years a lot of changes took place, for Darrington has never been a town to stand still. Almost all the streets were paved. A direct access road to town center was cut through, and the highway through Darrington became an alternate scenic route connecting Interstate 5 with the North Cross-State Highway. New stores were added to the main street. A comprehensive plan and a zoning ordinance made the town a community looking toward the future.

We liked Darrington. We liked small town life. We loved the

mountains surrounding the town. And, most importantly, we found friends there like none we had ever had.

Looking back on our first impressions of the long ride from Arlington, the smallness or non-existence of any neighboring towns, the desolateness of Darrington under an almost-raining sky, I see it could have been easy to decide not to stay.

But how much easier Paul and I had it than those who came to Darrington before us. And they stayed, too.

Ross and Eunice Hamlin came to Darrington in 1942. They moved up the Arlington-Darrington road in a little caravan. Ross went first, driving a gravel truck full of equipment for Jones and Anderson Logging Co., his employer. Eunice and Audrey Jones drove the family cars full of their belongings. A friend brought up the rear with a truck full of household effects. Bob Jones was caravan master. The road was gravel for most of the way, winding and narrow. It seemed a good deal longer than thirty miles. Eunice and Audrey thought it would never end.

In 1929, Dr. N. C. Riddle, the town's new physician, and his bride of a few months arrived in Darrington. How remote and small the town of several hundred people seemed, especially to Mrs. Riddle who had been assistant superintendent of nurses in a large hospital in Chicago. Dr.Riddle said his wife looked around town and was disappointed. But she took solace in the fact that there was a train depot and a track, a thin thread connecting her with somewhere.

Flora McCulloch Howe made the trip from Arlington to Darrington in a farm wagon. The year was 1900, only about ten years after the first settler arrived in the Darrington area. It took a day to get to Oso and another day to reach Darrington. It was summer and her family traveled from dawn 'til after dark. There were seven miles of puncheon road. The rest was dirt. At one point on that first trip the horses got bogged down in mud. Plunging in panic, they eventually tipped the wagon over, spilling out the meager household wares Mrs. Howe's family and her uncle's family brought with them to establish new homes away from the city.

Darrington's story, then, is not really my story — a latecomer up the Arlington-Darrington road. It is the story of the Flora Howes and Dr. Riddles and Ross Hamlins and many others who came to Darrington starting in the late 1800's to make homes where there were only mountains, forests and rivers. The land provided their means to live, and they settled down to the business of making a town. Until recently that town maintained a definite frontier feel and flavor, and its people lived with frontier flair.

But each new bridge, each widened, graded, paved section of highway has drawn Darrington a little more into the present and away from the frontier. Before it loses its sense of the past, I want to try to capture some of the history and color, the exuberance and pathos of the town as it was and never will be again.

Chapter 2

The Place and Its Native People

Darrington's setting is a spectacular *cul de sac* in the foothills of the North Cascades. It is approached along the lush valley of the North Fork of the Stillaguamish River and is bordered on the east by the north-flowing Sauk River. It is eighty miles from the bustle of Seattle, fifty miles from the county seat of Everett and thirty miles from Arlington, the closest town of any size. It is surrounded on three sides by the rich green of Mount Baker-Snoqualmie National Forest.

Although the town is only 549 feet above sea level, there is the feeling of being higher up than that. All around, except to the west of the town, are mountains. The most prominent mountain — and most beautiful — is Whitehorse (elevation 6,852 feet). Rugged, always snow-capped, forever changing in mood, the mountain dominates the town. Though the mountain is always present, no one with any sense of beauty becomes hardened to it. One cannot ignore Whitehorse.

"Have you seen the new snow on Whitehorse this morning?" a neighbor will ask.

"Can you hear the waterfalls on Whitehorse?" an old-timer will ask a newcomer at the time of the spring melt.

"Look at the stars hanging over Whitehorse!" I have exclaimed innumerable times to my husband.

When we first arrived in Darrington, someone jokingly told us that Whitehorse is the town's best weather vane. If you can't see the mountain, it's raining. If you can see it, it's going to rain. That saying is appropriate since one of Darrington's only drawbacks is its wet autumns and its wetter winters and springs. While Seattle's average yearly precipitation during a recent ten-year period was thirty-eight inches, Darrington's average yearly precipitation during the same period was eighty-four inches. Some of that heavy precipitation comes in the form of deep snow during some winters. Fortunately, the town lies on old river bottom composed of sandy, gravelly soil which drains rapidly.

We were also told when we moved to town that Whitehorse Mountain got its name from the shape of its highest peak which people claimed was roughly in the shape of a horse's head. Covered by snow, it always is a "white horse." We looked and looked until we too could see the form of a horse. But according to the late Nels Bruseth, a forester and amateur historian of the area, the mountain was named for another reason.

Fred Olds, a settler who came in 1895 from Michigan, lived near Whitehorse Mountain. One morning his old white horse wandered off and could not be found. As Olds searched for it, a neighbor called out to him — whether in jest or to be helpful, we will never know, "Fred, look up there on the mountain. Doesn't that patch of snow look just like your old *white horse?*" And so the mountain was named.[1]

For the Indians who lived here before any white man had ever seen the beautiful mountain, Whitehorse was So-bahli-ahli, "the lofty lady from the east."

Bruseth, who also was an artist, writer and friend of the Indians, retold the Indian story of So-bahli-ahli in his little book, *Indian Stories and Legends of the Stillaguamish and Allied Tribes,* published in 1926. Here is the story of Whitehorse and its neighbor to the north, Mt. Higgins, as Bruseth heard it from the Indians:

So-bahli-ahli (Whitehorse Mountain) was once a woman. She had come from east of the mountains. Near where she settled lived a man, Quay-hae-eths. She liked him very much, and he became her man, and they lived happily together, but this was not to last. Up from the whulge (Sound) came another woman, Ska-dulvas (Mt. Higgins) a young maiden of many charms.

She looked at Quay-hae-eths, envied So-bahli-ahli and decided to steal him. She dressed herself in beautiful colors, mostly red; smiled at and talked nice to the man. He made a move toward her! She suddenly grabbed him and placed him behind her. Then a battle began. The noise was terrific; hair flew all over the sky; rocks whizzed through the air, hit their mark, rolled down and made big rock piles down below. The battle ended in victory for Ska-dulvas, but she was disfigured for life by So-bahli-ahli who reached over and with her fingernails scratched those deep gashes across the face of her enemy. The man did not interfere the least in the battle. He just stood still and looked on. He stands there yet, the highest bald nob on the north east of Mt. Higgins.[2]

Mt. Higgins is another of the mountains visible from Darrington. It gets its name from Walter B. Higgins who pioneered a homestead near Hazel as early as 1887. Some local people imagine that the outline of a bearded Abraham Lincoln in repose can be seen in the uplifted strata of Mt. Higgins with the top of the head toward the west.

Other mountains which seem to cluster around the town of Darrington are North Mountain, Gold Mountain or Gold Hill, which rises abruptly from the Sauk River east of town, and Jumbo Mountain, a direct neighbor of Whitehorse, separated from it by Squire Creek. These nearby mountains give only a tantalizing hint of the mountain beauty that lies deeper into the North Cascades.

I have often tried to imagine what this area must have been like before the white man came to claim it from its original inhabitants. Immense fir and cedar were here. The forests were rich in game. Rivers teemed with trout, steelhead and salmon. Creeks and rivers were known to the Indians for the species of fish most common in them. The rivers and streams were also the highways for the Indians who used cedar dugout canoes for transportation.

Two of these canoes are part of a garden memorial to Nels Bruseth at the north edge of town. The larger canoe was carved by three Indians and Nels Bruseth in the backyard of his home. The smaller canoe is a racing canoe built by Kenny Moses, an Indian who makes his home in Darrington. A third canoe in the

18

collection was destroyed by vandals in 1968. It had been made by the late Jackson Harvey.

According to Indian legend, a long time ago the Indians did not live in the Darrington area. They commuted here, so to speak, from areas closer to the Sound. They came to hunt and to gather berries and edible roots in preparation for the winter. Their highway was the Stillaguamish River. Before the river turned north and away from their destination, they would turn their canoes into Squire Creek and, at a place a short distance from Darrington, would portage their canoes along a trail to the Sauk River. There they would again use a water highway to go to the Sauk Prairie, a wide, flat valley of rich earth northeast of Darrington.

Nels Bruseth told the story of *Saukwa Beault,* Sauk Prairie:

At one time Sauk Prairie was a big marshland and belonged to the Beavers. Indian tribes used to send out scouts to locate hunting, fishing and camping grounds. One of these scouts found what is now Sauk Prairie. In and around the marsh were many plants with edible roots, many kinds of berries, also much small game and birds. The scout had a vision of a great summer camp for his tribe. He wanted to secure the marsh for them and began dickering with the Beavers. They agreed to part with it for some pieces of hard wood with which to sharpen their teeth and with the understanding that thereafter the Indian should be friendly with the Beavers.

The scout brought his people up one spring. They thought it a wonderful place, and at once pulled out the dams which the Beavers had made, when most of the water rushed out. Then everybody went to work pulling out plants and bushes that did not have edible roots or berries, leaving all that had. Salmon berries, thimbleberries, huckleberries, spaykootlis (leek), etc.

This they did year after year, sometimes bringing in and planting new varieties. So in time Sauk Prairie became known far and wide for its wealth of good roots and berries.

The first fall after all the winter supplies had been prepared, meat cured, berries dried, fish and roots pounded together, all the Indians left for their homes down the river. The second year some of the people started gambling and became so possessed with the spirit of the sticks that they forgot to prepare for the trip down river, so they built winter houses and stayed over. Nobody suffered from want of food, because deer came right to their doors and there was fish in river and sloughs.

This started the permanent camps at the Prairie. More and more people came up the rivers. Those coming up the Stillaguamish crossed at Kuds-al-kaid (the Portage) a short distance below what is now Darrington.[3]

Early settlers found the portage trail between Squire Creek and the Sauk well-defined when they came. Years ago a road-building crew found a stone axe and indications of old firepits near the west end of Darrington Street. This area may have been a resting spot before the canoes were carried overland to the Sauk. At one time settlers considered calling the new town located near here by the name of Portage.

Despite the legend recounted by Bruseth which seems to tie the settlement of the Sauk Prairie north of Darrington with movement of Indians up the Stillaguamish River, the Sauk-Suiattle Indians who populated the area when the white man came were part of the Upper Skagit tribe of Indians. The Upper Skagits consisted of ten autonomous, extended villages beginning at Clear Lake near Mount Vernon and scattered eastward and northward along the Skagit River to Newhalem. The extended village of the Sauk-Suiattle, was called Sah-ku-mehu at the time of the Treaty of Point Elliott, January 22, 1855. It consisted of five winter houses extending from the mouth of the Sauk River to the Sauk Prairie with a summer house upstream near Bedal.

The Upper Skagits were not a large group of Indians. Estimates of population at the time of the treaty ranged from 300 to 880. The government chose 300 as a probable figure since the Indians were reduced by some seventy to ninety per cent in about 1825 through epidemics of smallpox and respiratory diseases. In 1934, O. C. Upchurch reported that the number of Skagit-Suiattle, or Upper Skagit Indians, was 205.[4]

The Sauk Prairie was one of the "free use areas" of the Indians. According to Edith Bedal, granddaughter of Chief John Wawetkin, it was the mingling place of bands of Skagit, Sauk, Suiattle and Stillaguamish Indians.[5]

The Indians who lived on the Prairie practiced a primitive agriculture, burning the ferns and grasses each year to prevent trees from growing up. The Prairie was a grassy turf with bracken ferns and berry bushes and wild rhubarb. It was rich with edible root and bulb plants such as wild tiger lily, wild carrot, and perhaps camas. The Indians only harvested the mature bulbs, leaving the young ones for another year. The white interior of the bracken fern root was pounded into flour. Fibrous plants from the Prairie were used to make ropes and fish nets. Baskets were made from cedar root or cedar bark or from willow. If a tightly woven basket were needed for carrying water, cooking or berry picking, it was made of cedar root. Loosely woven baskets for storing or carrying food were made from willow.

Fish were the main stay of the Indians' diet, and fish were plentiful in the Sauk, Suiattle and Skagit Rivers as well as in the many tributary streams.

Goat hunting was the job of the mountaineers among the Indians, according to Miss Bedal, and those skilled in hunting the wild goats were wealthy, because goat wool was very valuable. The wool was spun and woven into highly prized blankets. When the Indians couldn't get goat wool for blankets they spun together dog hair and the fluff from fireweed seeds and wove this yarn into coverings.

Blankets were also made from beaver hides which were cured, then cut into strips and twisted so that the fur was fanned out on all sides. Then the strips were woven together to make warm blankets with heat-retaining fur on each side.

Clothing possibly was made from shredded cedar bark, according to Miss Bedal, and items of clothing were also made from deer hides.

Some of the travelers among the Sauk-Suiattle Indians owned buffalo robes which they obtained when they went east of the mountains. Because her family was related to and had frequent contact with Wenatchee Indians, Miss Bedal's family had several buffalo robes.

Potatoes were brought to the Prairie early in the nineteenth century by Yak-bid, Miss Bedal's maternal great-grandfather. According to Miss Bedal, on one of his trips east of the Cascades her great-grandfather heard about the new vegetable which was obtained from the white people. The following year Yak-bid returned to the east with ten men. Each brought back a sack of seed potatoes which they planted in a communal garden. It took two seasons before there were enough potatoes to distribute among all of the Sauk and Skagit Indians. For several years the Skagits came to the Prairie to plant their potatoes, thinking that that was the only place they would grow. They soon found out that the potato could grow wherever the land was cleared and cultivated, and the potato patch became a part of almost every Upper Skagit Indian family's food supply.

For the Sauk-Suiattle, the dugout cedar canoe was the main form of transportation. However, Chief John Wawetkin brought horses over from Eastern Washington by the mid-1800's. Many Indian ponies were stolen by the early white settlers who merely fenced them in and claimed them as their own.

Apparently the Sauk-Suiattle never considered themselves party to the Treaty of Point Elliott which was signed in 1855. According to a statement made by William Moses, son of one of the tribal leaders after Chief Wawetkin became too feeble, the Sauk-Suiattle sent a representative to the treaty signing "just to find out what was going on." The representative, Skul-a-but-kud, never took off his hat and shouted, as did the other Indians after the signing of the treaty, so the story goes. This was taken as an indication that he did not accept the treaty. According to Miss Bedal, the Sauk-Suiattle never thought it was necessary to sign the treaty because they were not at war.

However, another Indian, Dahtl-de-min, who was identified as "sub-chief of Sah-ku-meh-hu" (Sauk-Suiattle) was a signer of the treaty with his X-mark. The treaty ceded all the lands from the coast of the Puget Sound to the summit of the Cascades — and that included all lands belonging to the Sauk-Suiattle Indians. This information apparently was either never known or never accepted by the Sauk-Suiattle Indians until the 1950's when they went to court to try to recover lands or money for lands they had lost to the white men years before.

The battle to keep their land was a long and losing one for the Sauk-Suiattle. Chief Wawetkin was friendly with the whites who established a trading post along the Skagit River. Early in his life he had worked as a mail carrier between Fort Whatcom (Bellingham) and Seattle and Olympia. But despite his cooperation with the whites, the distance inland that he and his people lived and the small number in the band, whites wanted the Sauk-Suiattle Indians off the land.

At one time some soldiers were sent up at the request of "unfriendly people" who lived along the Skagit. Their purpose was to drive all the Indians to the reservation. The Upper Skagits, including the Sauks, met the soldiers at the Baker River on the Skagit. When the white men could not prove that there was trouble with the Indians, the soldiers left and the Indians returned to their homes.

But there was an uneasiness abroad among the Sauk-Suiattle tribe. They wanted to make their claim on their homelands secure. They had faith in some of the white man's legalities, and they felt that if their land could be surveyed and its boundaries established, they could live at peace on their own land, unthreatened by white settlers.

Some of the accounts say that the Indians requested a survey, and that a surveyor was sent from Washington, D.C. William Moses gave this account to Miss Bedal in about 1950:

> When the white people came to settle on the lands there was a survey for the white people. They took the survey up the Sauk River, and they found a lot of Indians living along the Sauk River.
>
> The chief surveyor told the Indians that he was surveying the land from down the river up to there. As soon as he got there and saw all the Indians, he asked the chief about all the Indians. Then Chief Wawetkin answered him and said, "Yes, we are many Indians because we are two tribes, the Skagit tribe and the Sauk tribe."
>
> The surveyor said, "How would it be if we survey your lands for your tribes? I know it is your land where you have lived for a long time, but it better be surveyed for you Indians."
>
> Then Chief John gathered all the members of the tribe together and they talked it over and if all agreed they said it was all right to go ahead with the survey. Everybody agreed to have the land surveyed. The surveyors asked how far the lines of the land will extend, the boundary lines for the Sauk tribe.
>
> The Chief answered him and said, "It would be that we will use the Sauk River for the boundary line. The land on the west side of the river we will give up to the white people. The lands on the east side of the river to the summit of the surrounding mountains will be the land for the Sauk tribe." The land which the Indian gave up then for the white people is worth a lot of money. There is a lot of timber land and other good lands.[6]

The Indians provided six canoes for the survey party. They did not charge for the canoes because the survey was of their own land. They also provided axemen and chainmen.

According to Moses, the survey went up the Sauk river to Gold Hill where a corner post was established upriver a short distance from the present bridge. From that corner a line was run up Gold Hill to another corner post. Then the line ran north along the mountains towards the Prairie.

Somewhere between Gold Hill and Prairie Mountain one of the surveyors, a Mr. Hunter, from Washington, D.C., was killed in a fall in the rough terrain.

Hunter's death halted the survey. The chief surveyor, a Mr. Sheets, told the Indians that the survey was "almost finished" and that they could go ahead and build better houses on the land. The land was theirs, he said. But there was no legal title to the land. Chief Wawetkin went to Olympia and to the land offices in Seattle concerning the Indian lands, according to Miss Bedal. When the government responded by sending another man to finish the survey, white settlers on the Skagit intervened and the work was never completed.

Apparently the Indians felt that the "almost finished" survey gave them some security, for they began to build seven new lodges within the boundaries of the unfinished survey. Soon afterwards, white settlers began to come into the Sauk Valley. Miss Bedal estimates that settlement began in the 1880's.

Hard times hit the Indians about the time they finished their new lodges. They knew there was work at Puyallup picking hops. So the whole band took canoes and went to Puyallup to work. The trip was a long one, and the Indians were gone for a long time. When they returned they discovered that their new homes had been burned down. They went to the white settlers to inquire about their houses, but the white men said, "Get away from here, you Siwash." The Indians went to cut wood where they had always cut wood, but the whites said, "Don't cut that. It belongs to me." When the Indians went to claim their ponies which had been fenced in by the white settlers, they were told that the colts had jumped the fences and now belonged to the white men.

Evicted from their homesites, the Indians set up camps along the river bars — and waited. By this time Chief Wawetkin was old, and he was unable to do anything more for his people.

It was at this time that "Capt." Moses and "Chief" Jim Brown took over the leadership of the tribe. They decided to go to Olympia and plead the Sauk-Suiattle Indians' cause once more. They wanted land for their people.

The governor was sympathetic to their request and requested

a land grant from Washington, D.C. for the Sauk-Suiattle Indians. A month went by, and then the reply came that the land was granted and that a surveyor was coming to survey Indian land once again.

George Keeper came to supervise the survey. Joe McClair was the chief surveyor. Willie Barret was the chainman for the crew. Indian boys served as axemen, chainmen and flagmen. Indian pack horses hauled supplies and instruments.

This time the Indians chose land away from the Sauk Valley, up the valley of the Suiattle River. They hauled the surveyors in wagons to the Suiattle crossing on the Sauk River. From there Indian pack horses were put to work. Up the rugged Suaittle River course they went, beyond Tenas and Big Creek to the land the Indians wanted secured as their own. The survey took two years.

When the survey was completed, McClair told the Indians, "Now your land is surveyed, all that is inside the survey is yours, all the timber land, game, fish, salmon, all the berries. All this is for the Indians to eat. It is your own land but from this day it becomes your own again. From this day you go ahead and build your houses. You can cut the timber and sell anytime and you can get money from it to live on."

Capt. Moses replied, "From this time, this land which was mine from the beginning, it is like I was holding it in one hand and now since you surveyed it, it is just like I am holding it in my two hands."

The Indians built homes and started clearing the land. They cut shingle bolts and hauled them on horse-drawn sleds to the river where they were driven down to mills in the Skagit Valley. There were no roads into their settlement which was deep in the Washington Forest Reserve. Everything they couldn't supply for themselves they hauled in on pack horses.

However, within only a few years most of the Indians again would be homeless. In about 1915 one of the U. S. Forest Rangers, Tommy Thompson, told the Indians, "This land is not good for you Indians." According to Moses, Thompson made a report to the government that "the Suiattle country is not good land for the Indians. . . the Indians cannot live between the mountains. It would be better if this land is cancelled from the Indians." His report was accepted, and except for one or two families who had gained legal title to their property, the Indians again were turned out of their land. Once again they moved onto

Edith Bedal, granddaughter of Chief John Wawetkin of the Sauk-Suiattle Indians, studies the view from the cemetery on Sauk Prairie where her grandfather and other unnamed Sauk-Suiattle Indians are buried. Photo by the author.

the river bars and shifting islands of the Sauk, living in tents and makeshift shelters. While living there they secured an attorney in hopes of recovering their lands, but nothing came of their efforts.

After a time the Indians left the river and moved into some abandoned logging camp bunkhouses near Bennettville on the west side of the Sauk River. Little by little, the small band dispersed, looking for work and a place to live somewhere else.

In the 1950's the Sauk-Suiattle made an attempt once again to recover their lands or to get compensation for their land. That attempt was frustrated as well.

In 1960, in a joint petition with the other Upper Skagits, the descendants of the Sauk-Suiattle Indians finally were awarded compensation for their lands — at the value when they were confiscated. The total award to the entire Upper Skagit group was $426,801.[7] A ranch located on only 1700 acres of the Sauk Prairie and of the foothills beyond reportedly sold for more than one million dollars in 1973.

On a knoll within that ranch is one little piece of indisputable Indian turf. It is a small burial ground where Chief John Wawetkin was buried in 1912. Others of his village are buried there, too, for as whites began moving into the valley and crowding the Indians out, Chief John had suggested that his people move their dead from the scattered burial places along the river valleys to one place where they would be unmolested by the whites.

I stood in the burial ground in June, 1974 with Wawetkin's granddaughter. A broken down fence marked the perimeter. Only clumps of iris, phlox and peonies showed us some of the gravesites. Nearby an Angus bull bellowed and cows moaned. We looked out to the west across the pea fields and meadows of the Prairie, past the trees that mark the river's course and on to Whitehorse in its early summer magnificence. "The people sleep, looking out over the land and the mountains that were theirs," Miss Bedal said quietly, and somehow I felt like an intruder.

Very few Sauk-Suiattle Indians live in the Darrington area now. However, even into the 1930's large groups of Indians gathered on the Sauk Prairie for *speequods*, which would end in

Jimmy Price, left, and Leo Brown were participants in the Shaker funeral for Mary Smith, a Sauk-Suiattle woman who died August 1951 at the age of 95. The Shaker church met in Price's home on the Suiattle. Photo by Phil Webber. Courtesy of Alice Elinor Lambert.

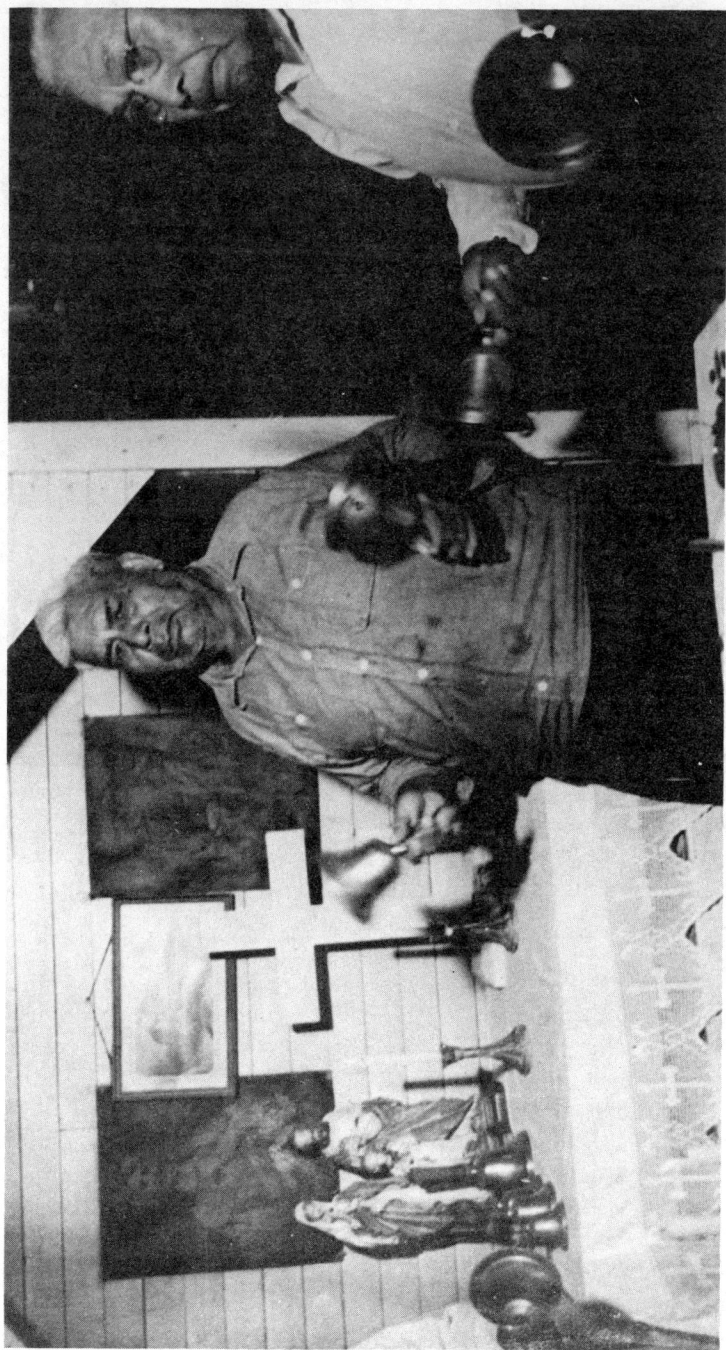

the traditional *potlatches*, or giving times, of the Northwest Indians.[8]

According to tribal custom, people were gathered for a *speequod* after one of the young men of the tribe had gone into the mountains to successfully search for the gods or spirits who would proclaim his life's work to him, teach him his spirit songs, and give him a spiritual awakening. His lonely spiritual exercise involved fasting, ceremonial bathing and patient waiting. Only after a young man had been visited by the spirits during this spiritual retreat could he lead a *speequod*. The celebration was essentially a proclamation to the Indian community of his spiritual rebirth.

The people would be called together for a meeting. Huge supplies of food would be brought together — salmon, berries, fresh meat; for this was a time for rejoicing, feasting, celebrating and sharing the spiritual gifts of the young man as well as material gifts of his family at the final potlatch.

The *speequods* which took place on the Sauk Prairie within the past 40 years were held on the property of Johnny and Martha Tommy. The land was originally allocated to Chief Wawetkin and his family at the time that most of the tribe moved to the Suiattle valley. The old chief was too feeble to make the move into the mountains and was granted a strip of land along the Sauk. The *speequods* were held in a smokehouse located on the property. The smokehouse has long been unused and recent snows have collapsed its walls.

Seventy-five to one hundred Indians would gather for several days of celebration there. White people were welcome at the meetings if they had no hint of liquor on their breath and if they did not disturb the ritual that took place.

Observers — both Indian and white — entered the smokehouse through a low door. They then sat down on rough benches which lined the room, facing the fire in the center of the room. Each person was given a set of *cha-howadi* [9], smooth, round sticks with which they could beat time to the music.

When all the guests were seated, the leader of the *speequod*, the young man whose spiritual rebirth occasioned the meeting, would begin to sing softly. Soon another man would pick up the refrain, singing in a loud voice for all to hear. One after another, the men would take up the chant, until the room would be full of the sound.

Near the fire, two men would sit holding the magic *tustud*,

Eva Brown, left, Martha Favin and Jesse Moses prepare salmon barbecue at Mary Smith's funeral, August 14, 1951. Photo by Phil Webber. Courtesy of Alice Elinor Lambert.

slender ten- or twelve-foot poles, which they would warm in the fire's heat. As the chanting grew, a faint quivering would begin in the *tustud*, slowly growing into a strong swaying motion. Apparently drawn on by the motion of the sticks and by the spirit they contained, the men would rise and begin to dance and sway, leap and run. When the first two became tired, other men would grasp the swaying sticks and continue the dance around the fire while the chanting and the beating of *cha-howadi* continued. The dance might go on for several days, with participants falling down exhausted to sleep fitfully on the hard benches while others continued to dance.

From time to time offerings of dried fish, meat, wool and baskets were laid on the fire. Other offerings to the spirits were laid near the fire to be given to the honored guests at the final *potlatch*, or giving time.

Also used at times at the *speequods* was the *Sko-deelich*, a hoop made from the magic sapling of vine maple or some other pliable tree four or five feet long. The sapling was bent into a hoop with the ends crossed, leaving handles about eight inches long by which it could be held by the dancer. Around the hoop on the outside was a fringe of fine, fuzzy cedar bark tied on with goat hair twine. This powerful hoop was less frequently seen by outsiders than was the *tustud*.

The *speequod* was an expression of the Indians' close relationship with nature and the power of the spirits within all living things.

Some of the Sauk-Suiattle Indians also adhered to what was called the Shaker religion. (The Indian Shaker religion should not be confused with the Shakers or "Millenial Church," a Protestant monastic group which arrived in the American colonies in 1774, settling at Watervliet, N. Y.) The Indian Shaker sect combines elements of Roman Catholicism, Protestantism and Indian religious practices. It was originated in 1881 by Squ-sacht-un, or John Slocum, a Squaxin Indian, after he reportedly died and was met at heaven's gates by angels who barred his entrance because of his wickedness. He was given the choice of either going to hell or returning to earth to change his ways and to teach his people what they must do to enter heaven.[10]

The followers of the religious sect were known for their

The meal at the funeral of Mary Smith. Photo by Phil Webber. Courtesy of Alice Elinor Lambert.

shaking or twitching during moments of high religious excitement and so were labeled "shakers" by non-believing Indians and whites. Leaders of the religious group at first were jailed and penalized in other ways by reservation agents who opposed the new religion.

However, the group was successfully defended by James Wickersham, a Tacoma attorney, who was retained by the Shakers as they sought acceptance on and off the reservations. Wickersham outlined Shaker beliefs and practices:

> . . . They believe in heaven as do the orthodox Christians; also in Christ and God, the Father of all; . . . they believe in future rewards and punishments, but not in the Bible particularly. They do believe in it as history, but they do not value it as a book of revelation. They do not need it, for John Slocum personally came back from a conference with the angels at the gates of heaven, and has imparted to them the actual facts and the angelic words of the means of salvation[11]

> The Shakers use candles, bells, crucifixes, Catholic pictures, etc., in their church and their ceremonies. As Mr. Ellis says, they use paraphanalia of the Catholic, Presbyterian, and even some of the Indian religion. They cross themselves as the Catholics do; they say grace before and after meals; they stand and pray and chant in unison, they set candles around the dead as the Catholics do, and believe in the cure of the sick by faith and prayer. In times of excitement many of them twitch and shake, but in no instance do they conduct themselves in so nervous a manner as I have seen orthodox Christians do at old Sandy Branch camp meeting in Illinois. They believe that by praying with a man or woman and rubbing the person they could induce them to join their church, and could rub away their sins, but they have no rite, no ceremony, no belief, no policy, no form of religion that is not in use by some one or other of our orthodox people.[12]

Shakers were known for their sober, upright living. "They make special war on drunkenness, gambling and horse racing, and preach honesty, sobriety, temperance, and right living," Wickersham reported.

Martha Favin supervises clean up work after the meal at Mary Smith's funeral. Girls are, from left to right, Nancy, Violet and Mary Harvey, one girl unknown and Patsy Brown. Photo by Phil Webber. Courtesy of Alice Elinor Lambert.

By 1893 the Shaker religion had spread throughout Western Washington where Wickersham said a majority of Indians "either belong or are in sympathy with its teachings." It boasted five church buildings, twelve ministers and 500 members in 1893. Shakers had also sent missionaries to the Yakima Indians east of the Cascades where a variation of the sect grew up called "the blowers."

The Shaker meeting house among the Sauk-Suiattle Indians in the last forty years was the home of Jimmy Price up on the Suiattle River. Now the closest Shaker Church to Darrington is on the Tulalip Reservation near Marysville.

Chapter 3

Explorers And Prospectors

The future town of Darrington was in Indian land. The mountains were a source of the Indians' spiritual strength. The rivers provided them with food and transportation. The forests supplied them with timber for their homes, cedar for their canoes, meat to eat and skins for clothing. The prairies were places where they could collect the berries of the seasons and the reeds and grasses with which to weave their utilitarian but beautiful baskets and mats.

But the white man saw the mountains, the rivers and the prairies as his for the taking, and he set out to explore this land and claim it for railroads and trails, for mining claims and for homesteads.

According to Nels Bruseth, the first white men to pass the site that later became Darrington were a party of Northern Pacific Railroad surveyors. The year was 1870. The party was headed by D. C. Linsley. With him were John A. Tennant, a resident of Whatcom (now Bellingham), Frank Wilkinson, H. C. Hale and a number of Indians who served as guides.

Linsley's job was to find a feasible railroad route through the North Cascades. The exploration started on May 25, 1870, in Whatcom. It ended August 3 in Seattle. In the intervening ten weeks, Linsley and his party logged 650 miles on foot, in canoe and on horseback, exploring and mapping country never before seen by white men.[1]

Linsley's route took him up the Skagit to the Sauk, then up the Sauk to the mouth of the Suiattle. He was determined to find out if there was a pass from the Suiattle Valley into Lake Chelan. His Indian guides protested that there was none; though their real complaint was that the trip would be too hard. Linsley convinced them to make the difficult trip by offering a thirty-cent-a-day advance pay for any canoe work they would have to do on the way up the valley.

After three days of canoe travel up the Suiattle, Linsley, Tennant and his Indian guides reached the end of navigable water. Sunday, they left the canoes and proceeded on foot. Soon they detoured into the Kaiwhat, probably the present Sulphur Creek, and began to ascend the creek valley. On the following Tuesday, the small party left camp at 4:15 a.m. to climb to the pass to Lake Chelan. The pass was about a mile and a half away, but it was three hours and fifteen minutes before the men reached it, following an old Indian trail.

On their return down the Suiattle, Linsley and Tennant left the Indians to take the canoe on down the river while the two white men hiked across the mountains separating the Suiattle and the Sauk to a camp established by Wilkinson. This camp was near the Sauk Indians' summer home, which was located near the present U. S. Forest Service Bedal Campground.

Here the men met the son of Chief Wawetkin. (In his diary Linsley identified Wawetkin as Chief Whometkan.) Most of the tribe were away on a fishing trip, but when they returned, the chief himself offered to guide the Linsley party over the Cascades into the Wenatchee Valley.

As Linsley made his way up the Sauk toward the pass, he dispatched other members of the party on several side explorations. Hale was given the assignment of going down the Sauk, crossing by a trail to the Stillaguamish River and proceeding down the Stillaguamish to the Puget Sound. He carried letters and dispatches to Governor Smith and home. He was also supposed to find out what had happened to $600 Linsley had requested from General Sprague and which was needed by Linsley before he began his explorations on the east side of the mountains.

Hale took three Indians with him. They probably descended

the Sauk to the point where the portage trail cut across the present townsite of Darrington, portaged to Squire Creek and proceeded by canoe down the Stillaguamish. However,Hale didn't get all the way down the Stillaguamish; his canoe was wrecked en route. In some manner unrecorded by Linsley, Hale managed to get to one of the base camps on the Skagit, obtain the needed money and return to Linsley all in a period of twelve days. That job done, Hale was dispatched again, this time to Seattle to obtain $1,000 and with instructions to meet the rest of the party on the Columbia River.

At the end of the exploration which took Linsley or members of his party up Lake Chelan, down the Columbia, along the Spokane River and finally westward again over the mountains by way of Snoqualmie Pass and the Cedar River, Linsley made recommendations for several possible rail routes:

A good route can be had from the foot of Rock Island, three miles below the mouth of the Wenatchee, to the Spokane River with fewer obstacles than between the "Sound" and the Columbia. Estimate of Route No. 1 from the mouth of the Skagit via Lake Chelan and the Columbia to the Spokane River about 50 miles below Lake Pend d'Oreille and 20 miles above the mouth of the stream. Distance, 326 miles. Cost $16,000,000 or $50,000 per mile.

Route No. 2, from mouth of Skagit via the Skagit, Sawk (Sauk), and Wenatchee rivers and across the "Great Plains" of the Columbia to same point on the Spokane as Route No. 1. Distance 347 miles. Cost, $13,000,000 or $38,000 per mile.

A line up the Steilagwamish (Stillaguamish) to Sawk (Sauk) summit would reduce the distance 10 miles and save $250,000 in cost. The estimate would then read: distance, 337 miles; cost, $12,750,000 or $38,000 per mile. [2]

If either Route No. 2 or its alternative had been used, Darrington would have been on the main route of the Northern Pacific Railroad.

Nels Bruseth mentioned in his notes that a second railroad exploration party followed the same routes and explored others in 1872. The second expedition was under the leadership of Thomas B. Morris. No other information has been located about this second exploration.

In 1881 a group of white men accompanied by Indian guides

38

reportedly came up the North Fork of the Stillaguamish River, used the Indian portage across to the Sauk, and proceeded downriver to the Skagit and back to the Sound. Less is known about these explorers than is known about the railroad survey parties. Years ago the Indians in the area recalled only that the men "shook dirt and water in pans."

It was the search for gold and other minerals that created the town of Darrington. In fact, it was the discovery of the mineral wealth at Monte Cristo, about thirty miles southeast of Darrington, in 1889 that gave purpose to an unnamed flat along the North Fork of the Sauk River which later became the town. In 1890 a group of prospector-miners headed by the Wilmans Brothers, began to explore the Sauk River to find a feasible wagon road route from Monte Cristo to the Sound. As soon as the route was marked out, construction began from the confluence of the Sauk and the Skagit at a place called Sauk City up the Sauk to Monte Cristo.

Sam Strom, who arrived in Monte Cristo in 1893 from Norway to work as a miner, wrote down a history of the Monte Cristo venture and experiences in the Darrington area for the benefit of Alice Elinor Lambert, a novelist who has made her home in Darrington since the 1930's. Strom's description of the building of the wagon road, which was later to be known as the Sauk River Monte Cristo Pioneer Trail, is a colorful one which bears repeating. I have only corrected the spelling and the punctuation where it is needed for clarity.

Work was first started on a wagon road at Sauk City on Skagit River up Sauk River to Monte Cristo about 45 miles away through mountains and forest all the way. The system of construction was a winding dirt road following the least resistance by avoiding the larger trees as far as possible. No gravel was hauled at any place. In swamps and soft places, puncheon split from trees on right of way was used, and this winding narrow road was pushed through to Monte Cristo or nearly so in the late fall of 1891.

Machinery for a sawmill was hauled in along with the progress of the construction of the road, that is. The machinery for the mill weighed many tons and was moved by horses, oxen and mules by relays as building the road progressed. This moving of the machinery and supplies to the established roadbuilding crews along the route was done entirely by the (word left out) known as freight crew, four and six horse teams and some oxen teams. Also some

The Sauk River-Monte Cristo Pioneer Trail is marked at Darrington by this symbol erected at the urging of Nels Bruseth in 1938. Photo by Elden Abbott.

pack trains to carry supplies to the front crews, the timber fallers and swampers cutting out the right of way and building bridges.

Thus it can be seen that the mass of machinery and men, horses, mules and oxen moved like a large caravan up the Sauk River chopping and blasting their way through and taking all machinery for a sawmill along at the same time. Thus it will be seen that the trail from Sauk City to Monte Cristo arrived there nearly all together, crew, bag and baggage and thus established the Sauk River Monte Cristo Pioneer Trail in 1891.[3]

For a year or two the trail was put to good use. A stream of prospectors, miners and camp followers moved up the primitive road. A favorite overnight camping spot for them was on the flats across from Gold Hill, the future site of Darrington. Here a cluster of buildings and tent shelters was hastily built to accomodate the travelers.

But the future town was soon to be bypassed. Further explorations, this time in search of the shortest feasible rail route, continued out from Monte Cristo. Barlow Pass was discovered, and the valley of the South Fork of the Stillaguamish River was considered a shorter route for a railroad. The railroad was completed in 1894, and the pioneer trail was abandoned except for local travel.

At the instigation of Nels Bruseth, a small historical marker was built at Darrington in 1938 to honor the builders and users of the pioneer trail. The monument stands at the first sharp curve on the road to Clear Creek. The marker is a concrete pillar representing a mine claim center stake. Inserted in it are an iron wagon tire used on the road, a pick used in the mines at Goat Lake and a miner's shovel. Rocks and ore samples from various mines in the district are cemented into the base. Carved into the base are the name of the trail and the dates of its use.

While some miners and prospectors were engaged in seeking their fortunes at Monte Cristo, others were busy on the mountains and hills surrounding Darrington and along the Sauk River. Certainly Darrington's future would be in minerals, these early prospectors thought. Between 1895 and 1900 these hopeful men had made 100 mining claims on Gold Hill alone. Claims in the area were made as early as 1890 by Soren Bergenson, Knute Neste, Charles Burns, George Knudson, B. C. Schloman, John Robinson and William Giesler.[4]

Up on Jumbo Mountain the Knudson Brothers had 17 claims in the area. Another area of claims there was called the Keywinder group. The group was held by the Bergenson brothers, Charles Burns, Knute Neste and George Knudson. Another group of claims, called the Hunter group, was owned by Charles Burns. Also on Jumbo were claims owned by James Smith, Charles Hudson, Martin Evert, James Elwood and John Spangler. These men had all found ores containing copper, gold and lead.[5]

Even Whitehorse, a favorite peak for weekend mountain climbers, must have teemed with activity for a few years as prospectors worked on their claims. On the east slope of the mountain were the Coffin and Mallet mines, owned by Samuel Nichols of Everett in 1906. These mines were said to be rich in gold, silver and lead. The Buckeye Basin on the northeast slope contained over twenty mining claims carrying copper, lead, gold, silver and other metals. Charles Burns owned the claims in the Buckeye Basin. Other mining claims were located in and around Wellman Gulch on the north side of the mountain and on the southwest side of the mountain.[6]

During the boisterous days of Darrington's mining fever, the town had a continual case of the jitters. Dynamite blasts boomed like artillery on the mountains. Experts came and went, pronouncing Darrington to be "promising," "rich," "the Klondike of Washington." Promoters journeyed in and out of the valley. Some were "capitalists from the East," "representatives from the wealthiest mining syndicate in Scotland," "expert miners from Germany" — most unidentified or unknown. They held out promises of investment, of smelters, railroads, big operations, a bright future for the little town.

The townspeople were on a see-saw of hope and disappointment, of big dreams and disillusionment. In 1902 one exasperated resident wrote: "The status quo, a chief feature of which consists of visits from experts and rumors of mine sales and smelter building is becoming monotonous, and citizens are hoping that something definite will transpire soon, if nothing more than the eruption of Mt. Whitehorse."[7]

Of all the prospectors and miners in and around Darrington in those early days just before and after the turn of the century, Charles Burns was the most visible and vocal. If others lost faith in the future of mining in the Darrington area, Burns didn't. He was prospector, miner, public relations man and businessman.

As early as 1895 he was campaigning for a railroad to Darrington. "No line of 35 miles in length can be built in the state that will develop as much wealth" as the Darrington route, he proclaimed in the December 19, 1895 issue of *The Arlington Times*.

"When the North Fork District of the Stillaguamish does open up," Percy Palmer, Snohomish County Assessor, declared in 1897, "it will be with a rip and a rush, and Snohomish County will see one of the greatest mining excitements ever known since the palmy days of '49. Charles Burns of Arlington is going to be the father of that country, and if he retains his holdings for a couple of years longer, it is safe to say that he will come out a very rich man."[8]

As some miners and prospectors abandoned Darrington for the hopefully richer prospects of the Klondike in 1897, Burns chided them for leaving and proclaimed that people ought to invest locally rather than in far-off propositions in the snowy Klondike. His faith seemed vindicated when in 1899 ore from the Blue Bird Mine on Gold Hill won first prize as the best copper ore exhibited at the Seattle Exposition.

The slightest vein of rich ore sent Burns out to find a backer. Once he announced that he had found some rich iron ore on his claims on Gold Hill. He was on his way out of town shortly after the discovery to try to find someone who would build a steel mill on the Puget Sound to handle his ore!

Burns was promoter and eternal optimist. He was also a working prospector and miner. He nearly blew himself up in a mine explosion in 1913 when a charge he had set went off prematurely. There was fear that old Charlie Burns had done his last prospecting. Apparently he hadn't.

The last mention of Burns was five years later when it was noted that he had been ill but was now recovered. Nothing else is ever said about the man who helped put Darrington on the map. Little else is known about him, either. He came from Ohio to Arlington before 1897 and then to Darrington in about 1898 or '99. He had a son Elmer, who lived in Mount Vernon in 1913, and who, according to Post Office reports, served as Darrington postmaster from 1901 to 1906. For a short time Burns ran a store, post office and hotel combination in Darrington opposite the train depot. That is about all we know, except for this: he never did get rich.

Neither did any of the others who worked in the tunnels that nearly honeycombed the mountains around Darrington, but hope continued — sometimes wanly — through the early 1920's and even into the Depression years. The pattern was the same: a rich strike; big talk about generating plants, tramways and a booming community; frenzied activity; disappointment.

Sometimes success came so close it seemed nothing could stop it. Once an assassin's bullet intervened between hope and sure success. This is the story of Jesse Benson Price.

J.B. Price came to Darrington in 1903 from the East to do some mining development work on Gold Mountain. Backed by his father, Attorney W.M. Price of Pittsburgh, Pa., the younger Price developed the Pittsburgh-Gold Mountain Mining Co. claims. There were eight on the north side of Gold Mountain and seven on the south side.

Price was no fly-by-night operator. He was thirty-one years old when he arrived, an engineering graduate of Western University of Pennsylvania (now the University of Pittsburgh) Class of 1894. He had served with the U.S. engineers in Spain and Havana, had been a division engineer during construction of the Wabash-Pittsburgh Railroad, and had been employed by the B & O and Illinois Central Railroads.

The young man set about an orderly development of a mine and smelter site. By the spring of 1907 he had done so much development work that there was promise that his property would be the first producer in the district.

A 300-foot wire suspension bridge with an 18-ton capacity had been built across the Sauk. One-half mile of connecting road, one-quarter mile tram road and one mile of haulage road from the mine to mill site plus the bridge provided the mine an outlet to the railroad at Darrington.

By July 1907 a smelter had been constructed on the mountainside, the first and last smelter to be erected in the district. A one and a quarter mile flume brought water from Seminole Creek to generate electricity for the plant which could develop 140-horse power and handle thirty tons of ore a day. Crushing and milling would be done by regulation machinery, but the finishing process was Price's secret.

Through the winter of 1907-1908, Price worked to get the smelter ready for full operation the next spring. It is possible that he ran some ore through the smelter to test it out. Then one late winter day, a stranger arrived in town. He asked directions to Price's smelter and found his way across the suspension bridge and up the connecting road to the new group of buildings that marked the smelter site. Price was in his office. His visitor knocked and entered. For several hours Price and J.H. Jahn talked quietly, warmed by the stove in the corner.

In1903 and 1904 J. H. Jahn had been indicted for crimes in Pittsburgh. The cases had been prosecuted by W. M. Price, Jesse's attorney-father. In 1905 Jahn had moved West. By chance he had met the younger Price in a Seattle restaurant that year. Jahn became a real estate man in Spokane. But he knew where Jesse Price was, and he planned to visit him someday and take revenge against the father through the son. March 4, 1908 was the day he chose.

After several hours of quiet conversation, Price's associate in an adjoining room heard a single shot from the office. Jahn walked out and into the next room. "I suppose you want me, too," the associate said. "No, I got the man I wanted," Jahn replied. He handed the man his gun. "I'm turning myself in."

Price's body was shipped to Pittsburgh for burial. His young wife left the pretty four-room house her husband had built for them and returned to the East. The smelter never ran.[9]

Many of the other mining claims on Gold Mountain, Jumbo and Whitehorse were small-sized propositions in comparison to Price's development. Some were merely stock ventures to capture gullible eastern money. But one mining venture near Darrington looked extremely promising shortly after the turn of the century. This was the Bornite Mine owned by the Bornite Gold and Copper Mining Co., Bangor, Maine. The mine was located about twelve miles south-southwest of Darrington up the Clear Creek Canyon. Considerable eastern capital was poured into the development of the mine starting 1903, but westerners invested, too. Charles D. Austin, Seattle, was one of the principal western stockholders and promoters. Between 1903 and 1910, the Bornite developers spent $300,000 on the mine near Darrington.

The area looked as if it would be a rich source of copper. A tramway with wooden rails capped with iron strips was built from Darrington to the mine. Horses in tandem hauled flanged-wheeled cars loaded with machinery up to the mine. A half-mile aerial span was constructed to reach the shaft opening across the

The swinging bridge across the Sauk was originally built by Jesse Price as a connection from the Pittsburgh-Gold Mountain Mining works to the railhead at Darrington. It was completed in the spring of 1907 and was washed out prior to 1921. Photo courtesy of Harold and Anna May Engles.

canyon from the tramway head. The finest in equipment — air drills, compressors, electric lights — was installed. At one time over 100 men were employed in the Bornite Mine project. Some 3,300 feet of tunnel were cut and blasted back into the mountain, but despite numerous encouraging reports to the contrary, no deposit of ore large enough for commercial development was ever struck.

In the spring, summer and fall of 1908, activity at the Bornite mine boomed. Two shifts of men were employed to keep drilling and blasting for the big vein. Things looked so good that a shipment of ore from there was anticipated for the spring of 1909.

However, in 1909-1910 activity slowed almost to a stopping point at the Bornite mine, perhaps a result of hard-money times. There was a shake-up in the management of the mine as eastern investors became impatient with the slow development and lack of ore. In the spring of 1910, primed with $60,000 raised in the East, the mine was scheduled to open up again, but it apparently never did. From then on the mine was maintained on a caretaker basis. L. W. Thiele was named resident manager in 1912. No mention was made again of the Bornite mine until August 1918 when *The Arlington Times* noted that Mr. Cull, engineer for the Bornite mine passed through Arlington on his way to Vancouver, B. C. Three months later there was this brief epilogue: "Mr. Stevenson of Sunset Mining Co. has hauled out most of the machinery from the Bornite mine." Some equipment was left to rust on the mountainsides. Years later, the Forest Service used two mule strings to haul out about 1,500 pounds of abandoned equipment, some of it salvageable for use by the Forest Service. Another dream had faded.

In the meantime, and for a time into the future Darrington had other mining hopes: Lime beds were discovered in 1913 between Darrington and Fortson, and Galbraith and Bacon Co. of Seattle announced it was going to build a cement plant eight miles west of Darrington. The North Coast Mining Co. planned major mining work on Gold Mountain, including an electric smelter. That was in 1915. Puget Sound Copper Co. started building a 400-foot tram bridge across the Sauk in February 1918 to reach low-level tunnels of ore. Plans were made for an electrical generating plant on Clear Creek to provide power for drilling and other purposes. Silver-copper ore in new strikes made by that company in 1921 were assayed at from $800 to

$2,000 per ton, and the American Smelter Co. expressed interest in building a smelter at Darrington to process the ore.

Though all mining activity in the Darrington area petered out in the 1920's and only flared for a brief time during the Depression, interest in the Bornite Mine was renewed in 1970 by Dean White, a former Darrington schoolboy, who formed the Bornite Exploration Co. White claimed the mine, situated on federal forest lands, by location under federal mining laws. In late 1973, White reported that the old tunnel had been reopened, a heliport had been built, outcrops of ore exposed and timber for two buildings had been ferried in by helicopter. He anticipated a diamond drilling operation in the summer of 1974, but illness prevented his work. Until he did some drilling he said he could not be sure of the prospects of reopening the mine for productions. By 1978 work there had not been resumed.

White's grandfather worked between 1918 and 1926 in a mine on Gold Mountain. Foreman was Sam Strom who had worked at Monte Cristo in its heyday. White apparently visited that mine operation as a youngster and became fascinated with prospecting-mining. His interest in the Bornite Mine was kindled as a boy when he and his uncle and grandfather went fishing up Clear Creek and camped at the lower tram terminal of the Bornite Mine. He reported that his grandfather thought it was a good mine, and that it was his opinion that the depression in 1907 had halted exploration work before ore could be located.

According to White, there are 3,100 feet of tunnel left and some of the old equipment is still left at the tunnel, overlooked by Stevenson and the U. S. Forest Service.

During the major build-up of mineral prospecting in the Darrington area, miners, prospectors and developers petitioned the Seattle and International Railway Co. to extend its rail line from Arlington up the Stillaguamish to Darrington. Up until the time the railroad was built, most traffic used the Skagit and Sauk Rivers and trails or wagon roads along the rivers as highways into the remote prospecting town of Darrington. Some freight was brought up a rough wagon road along the Stillaguamish as early as 1899, but both the Sauk and Stillaguamish wagon routes were long, tedious and expensive. The miners wanted a quicker, more efficient and cheaper way to get the ores they expected to mine to market.

Faced with the news that the Great Northern had let a contract for the extention of the Seattle and Northern Railroad from Hamilton on the Skagit River to Index via the Sauk River and Monte Cristo, the Seattle and International offered a deal to the Darrington area miners. If they would agree to let the S & I handle seventy-five per cent of their ore shipments for fifteen years, the S & I would build the railroad from Arlington to Darrington. The S & I intended to assure itself of riches from the mines. The Great Northern had its eye on Sauk River timber lands it reportedly owned or controlled. The miners agreed to the S & I's proposal, and in the summer of 1900 work began on the railroad.

With the start of construction there was no more talk of the Great Northern building a line through Darrington from the Skagit, and S & I crews tickled the speculations of the Darrington miners as they surveyed along the Sauk. The rumor was that the railroad just might extend through Darrington, up the Sauk and across Indian Pass to join with the Washington Central, a plan in which Linsley's alternative route would be followed.

Before the railroad construction to Darrington was completed, the Northern Pacific Railroad announced it had taken over the S & I. The announcement only fed the speculative fires that big railroad doings were in store for the fledgling town.

On June 5, 1901, the track-laying machine reached Darrington, and tracks were laid all the way to the depot, located in Block 8 of the Darrington Mining and Reduction Co. plat. Old Glory was raised to the breeze. Three kegs of beer were put on tap beneath it, and ham sandwiches were devoured by the track-laying crew and the homesteaders, miners and prospectors who quit work to join the celebration.

Either on that day or on July 1, 1901, when the first regular train puffed into town filled with railroad celebrities, a railroad official made a speech formally presenting the railroad to the town. Almost prophetically, it was a forester by the name of Smith rather than a miner who made the acceptance speech in which he spoke glowingly of Darrington's future.

The railroad's arrival was the biggest thing that had ever happened to the community. According to Lawrence "Toby" Freese, who was five and a half when the first train arrived, for many years the daily arrival of the train from "down below" was the occasion for everyone in town to leave what he was doing and head for the depot to see who was arriving, what supplies were being brought in, how much mail there was in the mail sacks,

While the Seattle and International Railway (later bought by the Northern Pacific) was being built in 1901, mail was carried between Arlington and Darrington by this bicycle rig that rode the newly laid tracks. The mail carrier was Joseph Chenier. Photo courtesy of Harold and Anna May Engles.

and what the Seattle papers had to say about the news of the world.[10]

The train made one trip a day for years, staying overnight in Darrington and returning the next morning to Arlington. Later it made a round trip each day, and still later a night train was added. After the mineral excitement was over and the green gold of the forests began to be mined, the train creaked and rumbled out of town every day loaded with fifty or sixty cars of huge logs, first cuts from the timber-rich hills and valleys east, north and south of town.

Today a single track still connects Arlington and Darrington. But the train does not come into town. Instead it is diverted north of town to the Summit Timber Co. mill where it picks up lumber, sawdust, wood chips and "beauty bark." Occasionally it carries a load of shakes from one of the small shake mills near town.

Passenger service on the line — which is now operated by the Burlington Northern — has long since been discontinued, and in 1967 the old depot that stood between Railroad Avenue and Montague Avenue at Darrington Street was burned down by the Darrington fire department.

For years the railroad was the town's main link with the outside world. Now the highway provides its major link. Trucks bring supplies to the town's stores. Mail is brought once a day from Everett by a truck driven by a private contractor. Trucks carry logs to the mills "down below."

Now the private automobile is the only way to get out of town. Some old timers still wish for the passenger train. And sometimes visitors to town wish the railroad still had passenger service, too.

Several years ago my father-in-law from back East came to see us. We picked up him and Mom at the Seattle-Tacoma Airport and brought them to Darrington in our car. After about a day in Darrington, the smallness of the town began to make Dad restless. The mountains around him made him feel trapped.

"Is there a train out of here?" he asked.

"Just a freight train."

"How about a bus?"

"No."

"Is there a car rental place?"

"In Everett."

"Then how do you get out of this place?"

"The same way you came in: by car. . . Or you can hike."

Dad stayed.

One of the engines on the Darrington or North Fork Branch of the Northern Pacific line shortly after the turn of the century. Photo courtesy of W. Ward Woodward.

Chapter 4

Early Mills

During those early years of mineral fever in the Darrington area, other enterprising people were already beginning to mine the green gold of the forests, developing an industry which would outlast the mineral craze and give Darrington a reason for existing for the next seventy years.

In 1901 one of the first trains into town brought sawmill equipment for Allen's Mill, known for some time as Darrington Lumber Co. and later as the U.S. Lumber Co. Mill. Within sixty days of the train's arrival, the mill was operating and continued to operate until about 1916. Allen's Mill was the first mill in town if you exclude a small mill that Austin Faulkner and Jack Montague installed out at the Squire Creek settlement a few months earlier.

The U.S. Mill was the largest employer within the town, competing with the Bornite Mine at the height of its development work. Both employed up to 100 men. Logging was done within a short radius of the mill. Logs were yarded in by means of a double-drum donkey and then were hauled to the mill by horses. Finished lumber was shipped out by rail. In 1902 the mill was producing 23,000 board feet a day. One of its early orders was for 150,000 board feet of railroad ties for the Burlington Railroad.

In 1910 the U.S. Mill owners created a furor in town by hiring twenty Japanese workers. Three years earlier one hundred Darrington people had signed a manifesto declaring that:

We, the undersigned, after full consideration and discussion, for the welfare of the people, positively refuse to allow Japanese or Chinese laborers to work in this town or vicinity with us or for us; therefore, we earnestly request every citizen, employee and merchant of Darrington and vicinity to cooperate by absolutely refusing said Japanese or Chinese laborers employment of any kind.[1]

How long the Japanese had been working for U.S. Lumber Co. is not known. However, at noon hour on Monday, June 13, 1910, about 100 men, hearing the pre-arranged bell signal, gathered at a street corner in town and marched to the mill. Ward Woodward recalled the episode in later years. "We all marched down to the U. S. Lumber Co. and rounded up all the Japanese workers," he recalled. "We took up a collection and paid their way out of town that day on the train." Three of the workers were allowed to remain behind to gather up the men's belongings. However, the Darrington men decided the Japanese were "lingering longer than was deemed necessary" and ordered the remaining men out on Wednesday. They left by foot.[2]

The episode attracted wide attention. The Japanese Vice Consul in Seattle, Kinjiro Hayoshi, undertook an investigation, and the U.S. Lumber Co. sought an injunction to protect the Japanese and the company's right to retain them. A hearing on the injunction was postponed indefinitely by Judge Black, and, as Woodward reported, "nothing more came of it."

The Arlington Times noted that the hiring of Japanese may not have been the only thing about the U.S. Mill bothering the Darrington citizenry at the time. In the summer of 1910, prohibition was due for a vote in the State of Washington. Incorporated towns and cities were to vote as separate units whether to be wet or dry. But unincorporated parts of each county were to be lumped together as one large unit, with the total vote in the county affecting every small, unincorporated settlement. Some Darrington residents had signed a petition requesting a special election to incorporate the town prior to the local option election in July, apparently with the intent of keeping the saloons open. The U.S. Lumber Co. brought a suit against the county commissioners enjoining them from causing the incorporation election to be held. Judge Black granted the request for an injunction, "basing his decision on the showing that the petition contained signatures of a number of persons not entitled to sign it, and that the territory proposed does not contain the required population of 300."[3]

It may have been out of frustration with the company leadership for ruining their hopes of keeping the saloons open — coupled with the current anti-Japanese mentality — that the citizenry chose to run the Japanese out of town. In the local option vote on July 5, Darrington voted 46-wet, 35-dry, but to no avail. In the county the vote was two to one to close the saloons, and that vote was the one by which Darrington was supposed to abide.

Another large and prosperous mill in Darrington in the early century was Charles Kane's mill on the Sauk River. In 1908 it was renamed Swastika Mill, and the swastika was the brand used to identify its logs. Kane had visions of great success and wealth in the shingle industry and built what Toby Freese called "an ingenious mill." Kane constructed a box crib 600 or 700 feet long in the middle of the river. At the head of an island there he built a four-log swing boom to guide shingle bolts from upriver into the crib.

One spring Kane employed a large crew of shingle bolt cutters upriver at Bedal. Against the advice of men who worked for him, he sought to float a huge drive of bolts downriver at one time. According to Freese, "He had so many shingle bolts in the river that he plugged the river up." The men broke up one jam only to create another one downstream. When the bolts got downriver, close to the crib and boom, they piled up again, this time ten or twelve feet thick. The river dammed up behind them and then let go like thunder. The drive swept through, taking the boom and crib. "Ten thousand cords of bolts went clear through to the Puget Sound," Freese recalls.

In 1909 Kane bought a large amount of cedar on the Sauk from the U. S. Forest Service, and the town buzzed with the implication of the contract. "It undoubtedly means that a logging railroad will be built up the east side of the Sauk," the January 30 *Arlington Times* announced. ". . . The mill will be the largest in the state." Kane announced plans to rebuild the mill, install a drag saw, two ten-blocks, a double block and upright.

Shortly afterwards surveyors appeared on the Sauk, and the town was atwitter with the possible meanings of the survey work. Was there to be an extension of the Northern Pacific Railroad? Was it a logging railroad survey? Was there to be a railroad to provide transportation for the Penn Mines at Goat

Lake? No one knew. A year later Northern Pacific announced its intentions of making major improvements on the Darrington branch. This announcement came on the heels of extensive rebuilding work which had been necessitated by winter floods. The announcement led to speculation that the line would become a transcontinental line. Darrington's hopes rose again, and the small mills flourished. But the time had not yet come for a logging boom.

Many small mills operated in the town in the early days of the century. One of the first was probably the Critchy Mill located on what is now Darrington street. Bloxham and Giles Mill (often referred to only as the Giles Mill) started operations in 1907 with twelve men employed. It was a shingle mill. Gomas' Tie Mill was located on the river flats south of the present Seeman Street. In 1908 the Iowa Lumber Co. was operating on the site that later would be known as the Washington Spar Works, providing spars for U. S. Naval ships. The little settlement of "Punkintown," located on the road to Clear Creek, was the site of the mill, and many of the houses there today started out as buildings for the Iowa Mill or Washington Spar. In 1910 the Darrington Cedar Co.'s Mill was being readied for operation, and the Hansley Mill was ready to resume work after a winter layoff.

It was common in those days for the mills to shut down from time to time for a month or more to wait for the right weather conditions so some more timber could be cut, or for the market to improve, or for railroad cars to be available for shipments. Sawmilling and shingle weaving — as the whole shingle cutting and packing process was called — were not steady businesses for a town to be brought up on.

By 1909 timber traffic on the Darrington branch of the Northern Pacific had increased to the point that a special night train was added to haul timber exclusively. The first run had seventy-two loads, and the train returned Sunday for more. Most of the timber at that time was being taken from lower down the Stillaguamish River at Oso, Hazel and Fortson. It would be a few more years before the big timber interests would run out of virgin timber in the lower valley and would begin cutting in the Darrington area.

While the town waited for timber to be cut elsewhere and for the big timber men to find the right time to begin logging in the Darrington area, the small mills were the town's only means of income. The newspaper noted each shipment of finished lumber or shingles with enthusiasm, but the writer also wished for more business. When Fortson Logging Co., about eight miles down the rail line, shipped ten loads of logs to mills on the Sound, the Darrington correspondent lamented, "Too bad we could not have these logs cut up in our own idle mill."[4]

During years that the shingle business looked promising, groups of twelve or fourteen shingle bolt cutters were hired to work up on the Sauk at Jim Bedal's, Valhurst's or Harry Gray's camps. "May this number never be less. Our town needs the business," the news writer editorialized.[5] But sometimes in those unstable years of the century's first decade, the bottom fell out of the shingle business, and bolts were stored in the mill ponds for months at a time until the market began to go up again.

It was a time of waiting for the little town, waiting not only for the rich ores that never materialized but for the big-time logging that would secure it a permanent place on the map and in the economy of the Northwest.

Chapter 5

The Settlers

It is difficult to say exactly who was the first settler in the immediate vicinity of what was to become Darrington. Prospectors came and went. Some lived on their claims. Others lived down in the flats between the mountains and the rivers.

According to Stacy B. Emens, the first bonafide settler near Darrington was George Slater who came in 1890. Emens, D. C. Knapp and William Ray came about the middle of February, 1891. They had their supplies brought up from Hamilton on the Skagit River by Indian canoes. Apparently the men hiked the route, for Emens recalled in a letter to Nels Bruseth in 1939, "We called it fourteen miles, and it was all of that as we had only a surveyor's line to follow most of the way."[1]

A few months later, on July 20, 1891, the people in the area applied to the U. S. Post Office Department for a post office of their own. Up until then they had been supplied with mail sporadically by the Mansford Post Office, ten miles north of Darrington in Skagit County. The population to be served by the proposed post office was sixty-five, a figure which surely must have included every miner and prospector on every hill around.

The Alex McCulloch family homesteaded at Squire Creek in 1900. Left to right are Beulah, Flora, Grandmother Jeannette Faulkner, Donald, Cora Bell and Alex. Photo was taken about 1904 or 1905. Courtesy of Flora McCulloch Howe.

In order to apply for postal service, the proposed post office had to have a name. There is one basic story about the naming process with two sets of details. In a letter to Nels Bruseth in 1939 Stacy B. Emens said the naming took place in this manner:

A naming committee was formed consisting of J.C. and C.L. Laplant, G.F. Slater, Everett Bordon, C.D. Knapp, William Ray, W.W. Christopher (sometimes referred to in Bruseth's notes as Christopherson) and Emens. Knapp suggested the town be called "Norma" after his daughter. Christopher volunteered the name of "Darrington", his mother's maiden name. The committee voted and the result was a tie.

Unable to break the tie vote, the men decided they would accept a chance vote. On one side of a piece of paper they wrote "Norma"; on the other side they wrote "Darrington." Before they threw the paper in the air they agreed that whatever name appeared face up would be accepted for the town's name. "Darrington" turned up, and so the post office and town were named.

Knute Neste, pioneer prospector in the area, gave a different account of the naming process in an article in *The Arlington Times* in 1921. Neste claimed that he, Stacy Emens, Warnick, Slater and Smith were on the committee and that the vote was split between the names of Darrington and Portage. He said Darrington was a modification of the name of Bellington, a teacher at the school, and was suggested by the *daring* required to live in that wild country being named. Up until then the place they were naming had been known as Sauk Portage or The Burn. He said that at the final vote, someone put Darrington on both sides of the slip of paper.

Whatever the process was that secured the name of Darrington, the town was named and it was granted a post office. The town's first postmistress was Carrie M. Hile, appointed January 28, 1892. Mrs. Hile's husband carried the mail, bringing it from the Mansford Post Office on a regular basis. The post office was in the Hile home, west of the present town limits, near Kirk Lake and out towards Squire Creek. At that time it was centrally located among the scattered homesteads and mining claims in the area.

Other postmasters and postmistresses have been John Knudson, appointed December 7, 1895; Isabel F. Olds, appointed November 20, 1899; Elmer E. Burns, appointed November 21, 1901; Charles E. Moore, appointed May 7, 1906;

William Ward Woodward, appointed February 26, 1917; Mel LaHammer, appointed January 1, 1966; Virginia Howard, appointed 1967 on a temporary basis; and Verner Hoglund, appointed permanently in January 1971.

There were quite a few homesteaders in the vicinity of the post office before 1900. In 1890 and '91 Mat and Charles Niederprun, political expatriates from Luxembourg, settled homestead claims out near Squire Creek. Others in the area were Jim Smith, Austin Faulkner, Vet Smith, Henry "Old Man" Miner, John Spangler, Eli Pacqui. In 1895 Mr. and Mrs. Fred Olds settled near the Hiles' place, eventually buying Hiles' homestead rights and making considerable improvements on the place.

Fred and Isabel Olds had been married only a short time before their arrival in the Darrington area in 1895. Their only child, Oliver, was born in their homestead cabin. In 1900 Fred Olds died of tuberculosis. His funeral was the first one recorded in the fledgling town. Neighbors made a coffin of cedar and buried him near his home. Austin Faulkner, then a newcomer to the Squire Creek area, read a Bible passage over the grave. Others attending the funeral were E.J. Miles, Stacy Emens, Mrs. Olds and Oliver. Olds' grave is marked by a small boulder into which has been scratched his name and the year of his death. The simply marked grave is just a few feet from the south side of the county extension of Darrington Street, west of the town limits. Some children who live nearby had to guide me to it. I would have thought the headstone was a common rock and would never have stooped close to read the simple inscription. Next to the marked grave is another small mound which the children told me must be the grave of Olds' child, but I do not know if Oliver followed his father in death shortly afterwards. Mrs. Olds stayed in the area only a year or two after her husband's death, and then remarried and left Darrington.

The people who homesteaded out near Squire Creek lived in a spectacular place, nestled in at the feet of Whitehorse and Jumbo Mountains, supplied with water by a clear mountain stream and surrounded by great forests. It was a cool place to live in summer with cold air circulating downward from the snowy places on Whitehorse or from Squire Creek canyon between Whitehorse and Jumbo. In the winter it could be an extremely cold place to live, but the settlers didn't seem to mind.

I am writing this today only one hundred yards from Squire Creek. When the door of the spacious log lodge in which I write is opened I can hear the creek in conversation with itself. The early spring melt is past, and for two months now we have had no rain. But the creek still runs — subdued a little, but clear and cold as always, running deep and quiet in places and churning and bubbling over rocks in the shallows. The creek is changing course here. It has left a deposit of tumbled boulders on this side of its channel and has begun to eat away at the sandy bank across from these acres of land. It is a living creek, changing its depth according to the season, changing its course according to some unknown whim.

The big picture window in the house which has been loaned to me for a writing retreat frames Whitehorse Mountain. It is a moody mountain today, burdened with heavy clouds that slip down its steep sides, envelop its crags and fill its snow basins. Somehow the gloominess of this cloudy but rainless day seems to bring the mountain closer to the house than it actually is.

As I sit here I try to imagine what it must have been like to live on this creek and in the shadow of Whitehorse seventy years ago. There would have been quietness here — more quietness than is here today, for in the distance I can hear the hum of log trucks on the highway and the drone of forest fire-spotter planes above me.

There would have been constant work here, too, for in this clearing where I sit today, there is evidence of the forest's effort to move in again. If I were to try to cultivate this land it would be hard work, and in this dry summer, how much water would I have to bring by bucketsful from the creek to keep my valuable garden from dying of thirst? How soon would I have to begin to worry that frost might kill my bean plants before I had the second harvest from them? If I needed staples from the store in Darrington, would I hitch up my horse today and ride the three miles to town, despite the threat of rain and the ominous roll of thunder I hear among the mountains? Would I have made it as a pioneer? I don't know. But I have met people who did make it as pioneers right here on Squire Creek.

One of them is Flora McCulloch Howe whose family moved from Ballard near Seattle to Darrington in 1900. She was six years old when her family arrived here by wagon, and she remembers with warm feelings the pioneer days here.[2]

Flora's father, Alexander, her mother, Cora Bell, and sister and brother, Beulah and Donald, moved into their one-room cabin west of Squire Creek in the spring of 1901. That same spring Uncle Austin Faulkner, who had come to Darrington with the McCulloch's, moved his family into a neighboring cabin. Both families had spent their first Darrington winter as guests in Mat Niederprun's homestead east of Squire Creek. Whenever the weather had allowed, the two men had worked on their cabins during the previous summer, fall and winter in hopes that the families could be housed by spring.

The cabin the McCulloch's were to call home was one large room made of logs, heated with a stove and wood heater and furnished sparsely. There were beds at one end of the room, cupboards at the other. The only other furnishings were a table Mrs. McCulloch brought with her from Ballard, two handmade chairs, a moth-proof chest McCulloch made and which his daughter still has, and a box for son Donald to sit on. Later a rocking chair was added to the furnishings. "That was because Grandmother Faulkner came to see us every summer, and that was supposed to be her chair," Mrs. Howe recalls. Later a loft with a ladder for stairs was added to the cabin and became the two sisters' private domain.

It was difficult farming the newly cleared land in this wild country where the forest begins to grow back as soon as you cut it down, and Austin Faulkner soon gave up trying to make a living from the land. He and his family returned to Ballard shortly after moving into their new Squire Creek home.

But McCulloch, "a frugal Scot", according to his daughter, stayed on. Somehow he found ways to make ends meet. He received a little income from the hardware store in Ballard which he had owned and operated for years and which he now rented. He had a little money in the bank. But the rest of his and his family's livelihood came from the land around them.

"We had chickens, pigs, between one and four cows, a beef or two to butcher each fall," Flora recalls. The family raised potatoes and other vegetables for their own use and to sell. "As I got a little older, that was my job, to peddle vegetables in town," Flora remembers. She sold the vegetables from a two-wheeled cart pulled by Nellie, the family's horse.

To get to town and back Flora had to ford Squire Creek. That was okay when the stream was low as it is this summer. But when the creek was high, Nellie would have to swim across, and water would start to come through the floor boards. Flora would put her feet up on the dashboard to keep from getting them wet and hang on as tightly as she could to the reins and to her seat. "I was really scared," she remembers.

What the family could not grow on the farm was purchased at Montague and Moore's store in Darrington, about three miles away. Flora said you could never be sure whom you'd meet on a trip to or from the store. She recalls seeing a cougar on a fallen tree across Squire Creek just as she was mid-stream on an adjacent footlog loaded down with a ten-pound sack of meal and the day's mail. She kept her balance and made it to the home shore. The cat kept his balance, too, and kept going wherever he was headed, which was in the opposite direction.

Meeting a cat, or some other wild animal, wasn't an unusual occurence in those days, but you can imagine my husband's and my excitement when we scared up a young cougar while hiking near Squire Creek in recent years not far from Flora Howe's meeting place with a cougar. A flood of feelings poured over us as we watched the small cat scamper lightly away from us and up an embankment.

Flora Howe's father had moved to the Darrington area because of ill health and on orders from his doctor. He was forty-four years old the year he settled there. Apparently the tonic of the mountains and streams and the pioneer life agreed with him because he died in Darrington at the age of 101.

One of the Squire Creek settlement's most colorful characters was Fred Fuller. Fuller was an Englishman. Some people say he had been in the British navy and jumped ship in Seattle. He first came to Darrington in 1897 as a book seller, peddling a book about the Klondike. About 1900 Lord Fred, as he was called, settled on a homestead on Squire and Brown's Creeks. The one-man settlement he developed was a source of news and legend for years.

A tinkerer at heart, Fuller built a self-sufficient home in the wilderness. A little sawmill which he constructed for sixteen-and-a-half cents provided lumber for his home and outbuildings. His own blacksmith shop provided him with whatever metal things he needed. The forge was blown by a fan fashioned from

————————————————————————➤

The original Montague and Moore store in Darrington, built in 1900, consisted of a cluster of buildings including a barn, warehouse-boarding room house, butcher shop and log cabin store. Pictured left to right are Charles Moore, storekeeper; Ward Woodward, his nephew; Edith Woodward; Frank Webster, delivery man; Shep, the delivery man's dog; and Hipes, the butcher. Photo was taken about 1907. Courtesy of W. Ward Woodward.

the works of an old bicycle. A Dutch oven of his own design kept bread rising at a constant temperature. His small farm provided food for the year. He canned a good supply each summer. He hunted for his meat and for adventure, sometimes bagging three cougars in one hunt, a feat which was considered praiseworthy in those days. His shirts were made from flour sacks. His home was papered with magazine pictures and butterflies. He developed a contrivance to take out weeds by the roots but advertised in the newspaper for ideas on how to rid a place of skunk cabbage.

Radio was his hobby, and he helped two Darrington boys, Joe Keenan and Paul Woodward, build their first radio sets. His own radio was a tangle of wires and a tube, but it worked.

Fred never married. He was one of the fifty-eight "Jolly Bachelors" who turned up for dinner parties, dances and literary society meetings in the tender years of the century. At one time his bachelor buddies feared that he was going to desert their ranks, for he was busy improving his house, a sure sign in those days that a man intended to bring home a wife. But instead, Lord Fred was just making the place more presentable for his spinster sister who came to stay with him for an extended visit..

Fred Fuller died in the winter of 1949-50, apparently of heart failure, as he attempted to shovel a path from his homestead to town, a distance of several miles.[3]

Chapter 6

School Bells
In the Valley

Darrington's first school was out toward Squire Creek. It was built on Hile's place probably five years before the McCulloch's located in the area. Neighbors pitched in and made the small structure out of native materials. Only the window glass was imported from the outside world. Henry Miner made the desks, chairs and tables out of heavy cedar slabs, designed to withstand heavy use. The settlers took a census of school-age children, and, stretching the facts a little, came up with a large enough number to warrant sending out for a teacher. A man from Snohomish by the name of Jones was hired for the post. When school opened there were four students.

The school population grew, and the little cabin school house on the Hile place became too small to house the students. A second school house was constructed, this one farther west toward Squire Creek on what is still called the Whitehorse Farm. By 1901, the newly completed railroad was drawing more settlers into Darrington, and the center of population began to shift. The second school house was abandoned in favor of one located in the town of Darrington on the east side of the what is now called Emens Street across from the Darrington Store.[1]

Toby Freese tells the story about the first attempt to hire a teacher for that school. A school board consisting of Charles Moore, Toby's stepfather, Fred Freese, and John Knudson was appointed to find a suitable mentor for the town's children.

Anxious to find one as quickly as possible, two members of the board wrote out for teachers, telling anyone interested to catch a train to Darrington to have an interview. If they were satisfactory, they could just stay on in town. Much to the board's embarrassment, two teachers responded to the letters by arriving the same day on the same train. The community had planned to have an impressive party for the prospective teacher when she or he arrived, so the board courteously told the two young women that they would *both* be feted at a party that evening and housed at one of the boarding houses for the night. The next morning the board would inform them which one had been chosen to be teacher. This arrangement was made so that the teacher who wasn't chosen could catch the morning train out of town.

The party went well. So did the usual drinking bouts at the town's three taverns. (Freese estimates that there were only about thirty people living within the present town limits in the year 1901, but already there were three taverns, one being a tent tavern at the corner of Darrington Street and Elwell Avenue.) One of the townsmen proceeded to get very drunk that night. Stumbling around in the dark he fell into one of the very primitive privies. Some of his drinking buddies dragged him out, but before they could get him cleaned up, he had staggered into the boarding house where the two young lady teachers were staying. "He perfumed the place up a bit," Toby recalls with a mischievous twinkle, "and, by God, the next morning *both* those teachers left town on the morning train."

Apparently there was a good supply of teachers in those days, because despite the unhappy experience of the first two applicants, the town soon was able to hire a young woman by the name of Miss Hall to teach the first classes in the Darrington school.

For some of the small children who lived out near Squire Creek, the long trek into town to attend classes seemed too long and dangerous. One of the children who did not attend the first

One room of this school building was constructed in 1904 at the corner of Riddle and Madison Streets. The second room was added in 1905 or '06. Photo from Darrington District Ranger Station historical files.

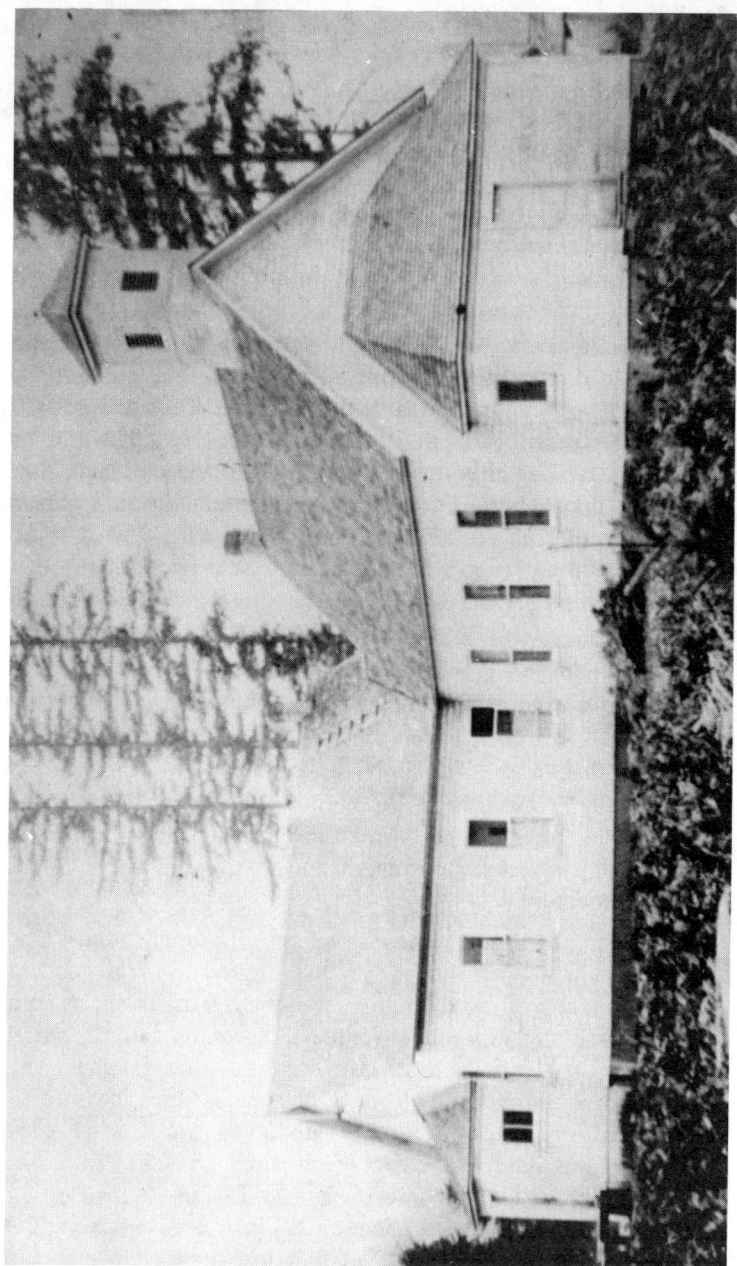

school in Darrington was Flora McCulloch. Instead she was sent to Ballard to live with her grandmother during the school year while she completed the first, second and third grades.

By the time Flora was ready for fourth grade brother Donald was ready for first grade, and Flora was allowed to drive herself and brother to school in the little cart she also used to deliver vegetables. By this time, 1904, the school population had outgrown the first schoolhouse in town, and another one had been built at what is now the corner of Riddle and Madison. A year or two later a second room was built onto the school, and for the first time two teachers were hired.

In 1907 a young teacher came to town whose teaching and life were to have a life-long impact on the group of students he taught. The young man was Newton Castle Rhoads who was twenty-three years old when he came to town. He taught in town until 1913. He was hired to teach grades four through eight, but he took it upon himself, without further remuneration, to teach three years of high school work to students who wanted to go out to accredited schools for their senior year in order to get a high school diploma.

The influence of a good teacher is never lost. Of eight students whom he groomed for high school graduation, five went on to normal school and some of those five to university training. All five of them came back to the Darrington area to teach school.

For Toby Freese, who quit school at the end of eighth grade, it was the fact that he had been Castle Rhoads' student that got him into high school several years later in Arlington where he was driving school bus.

According to Freese, Rhoads was an all-around man, "One hell of a man, to put it bluntly," he recalled. He was good in athletics and encouraged his few students in many sports and games — some of which he invented to accommodate the small number of students he had. He was a photographer who specialized in farm family and farm scenes which he sold to supplement his teacher's salary. He loved music, and even though he was not required to teach music, he did. Toby has searched in vain for the song book that Rhoads used. Puffing contemplatively on his pipe one evening Toby began to recite the words from some of the songs in that lost book, remembering snatches of two or three including one which went:

My heart is not here;
My heart's in the highlands
Tracking the deer

It was with this remarkable teacher's encouragement that the older students formed the Darrington Literary Society. The society, which included both boys and girls, put on a monthly entertainment consisting of plays — some original, some not; recitations, poetry reading and comedy routines. The show was attended by everyone in the town and its environs. The society put out a little "newspaper" and members read parts of it at the monthly entertainment.

In the paper the students poked fun at some of the townspeople. It got so that people came to the entertainment to see "who's going to get it tonight." Toby remembers two "pokes" from one issue of the paper when it was edited by Flora McCulloch.

Gust Lundquist was a rather unkempt bachelor prospector who was known for not relishing baths. But Gust always attended the literary society performances like everybody else. Flora read from her paper that Gust was waiting for Charlie Moore (the storekeeper) to have a sale on soap. The not-so-covert message was not lost on Gust. The next day he appeared in town all spic and span, again proving the power of the press.

Another poke was made at Fred Fuller, the very self-sufficient homesteader from Squire Creek. Occasionally Fred would come into town to get tanked up at the taverns, reportedly having learned to enjoy his brew as a sailor in the British navy. Fred had a crippled horse, "an old probate," Toby called it, who had trouble keeping his footing on a return trip from the tavern one day. With his horse down in the dust, Fred ranted in drunken confusion from his wagon perch, "Get up, you old thing, or I'll run right over you."

Even after Rhoads left Darrington he continued his interest in his proteges. At a teachers' conference a few years later he met Pearl Towne, who was a new teacher at the time. Putting his arm around her, he escorted her up and down the aisles, introducing her proudly to the others as one of his former students.

In October 1918, Rhoades who was now superintendent of the Sultan grade and high school, invited his five teaching students for a reunion at his home. Only a few days before they were to get together Rhoads was taken ill with influenza and died.[2]

Teaching in a one- or two-room schoolhouse seems like an impossible task to those of us who have known only the multi-roomed institutions of our communities today. Learning in a single classroom school also appears to us to have been a feat of major proportions. But Pearl Towne Reece says that neither the teaching nor the learning was that difficult. She taught in four of the one-room school houses in the Darrington area after graduating from normal school in 1917. Older students helped younger students in their subjects. Students learned to concentrate, being able to read silently to themselves as she instructed other classes orally. Discipline was no problem. Students knew that if they didn't mind the teacher they would be answerable to their father's switch when he found out about their misbehavior. In most of the one-room schools in which she taught Mrs. Reece had fifteen or twenty students. She figured out once that she had to prepare sixty lessons a day to meet her students' needs. The lessons included the three R's plus geography, history, physiology and other subjects at all eight grade levels.

The last year she taught in a one-room school was 1928. That year she taught all eight grades at the White Pine School on the road to the Sauk Prairie. The school house with some additions was later to become her home for thirty-six years. In 1949 Mrs. Reece returned to teaching and taught for thirteen or fourteen years, this time in the multi-roomed, new building in Darrington. She preferred teaching in the earlier days when, to keep warm on a wintry day, everybody gathered around the big iron stove and kept right on with the lessons of the day. [3]

The days of the one-or two-room schools in the Darrington area were numbered as the school population grew and bus transportation became feasible. [4] By 1923 a new multi-room grade school was built on the east side of the block now occupied by the Darrington Elementary School. The old two-room school was bought by Olaf Tronsdale for $50 and moved to the corner of Alvord and Madison where in 1978 it still

-->

Students at the White Pine School out toward Sauk Prairie in the late 1920's included, front row, left to right, Artis Reece, Betty Reece, Joann Reece, Unice Scott, Ronald Adam, Alvin Adam, Eddie Reece, Arvol Hyatt. Second row, left to right, Edith Scott, Frances Long, T.W. "Dub" Lewis, Louis Smith, Lewis Scott, Jim Thompson, Doris Long. Third row, left to right, Jack Long, Cecil Smith, Walter Bates, Morris "Shorty" Long. Back row, left to right, Elizabeth Smith, Nellie Lewis and Bobby Thompson. Photo courtesy of Bert Hyatt.

served as a private home. The old high school was built in 1925 or 1926 on the same site as the grade school for a sum of $18,000.

At the same time, however, the Darrington district ran two outlying grade schools, Whitehorse (or Fortson) school near where the Whitehorse Community Center was in 1978; and the White Pine School out toward Sauk Prairie. High School students were bussed to Darrington and in 1930 the White Pine grade school students also were bussed into town. The Whitehorse School continued to operate into the 1950's.

By 1929 the high school building built three or four years earlier was inadequate in size and equipment, according to state standards. In the midst of the Depression, the district tried to pass and failed two bond issues to build another high school. At the same time the school district was in an upheaval. There was dissension in the community over the selection of a school superintendent and the running of the school. Three board members had resigned during one school term, one at the time a superintendent had been selected for a two-year term. According to a report from W. F. Martin, secretary of the state board of education, the high school facilities were "inadequate" and teachers "inexperienced." "Altogether the school is in bad shape," he wrote. He recommended conditional one-year accreditation upon "satisfactory reorganization of the school."

School board and district citizens apparently pulled themselves together to face the challenge. By 1936 the district had rallied to the schools' support. A federal Public Works Administration grant of $22,909 along with $14,000 from the state and $20,000 raised locally through a special levy made it possible to build a new high school. Total actual cost was $51,462.20. That "new" high school was still a part of the "old" elementary school thirty-seven years later — and the subject of fire marshal's and building inspector's complaints and threats. But in 1936 it was a fine building, with adequate rooms and equipment for a high school population of seventy or eighty students.

In 1932 the old Darrington District 319, which had included the two outlying grade schools, consolidated with a district in Skagit county and became the Darrington Consolidated District 330. Now high school youngsters from the Prairie and from Bennettville were bussed to the central school in town.

The Depression hit Darrington hard. A reflection of the difficult times is found in brief notes in the school board minutes from those years. In the 1932-33 school year, teachers' salaries were reduced by ten percent from the previous year. In 1933 bus drivers — who were getting about $140 to $160 a year in 1929 agreed to take a reduction in pay and keep driving. In May 1933 a janitor's position was open at the school. Twelve men bid on the job. Low bidder — and the man who got the job — was Earl Jackson at $35 a month for ten months. Highest bidder had bid $80 a month. In 1931 all teachers and school employees pledged a portion of their salary each month for a community relief fund. The $90 a month was administerd by Dr. B. T. Blake, Dr. N. C. Riddle, Art Anderson, Ward Woodward and Tom Long.

In 1958 a new high school, constructed on the south side of town, was opened to a growing high school population. The old high school with new additions continued to function as an elementary school. All the small schools in the area were closed in the 1950's and all of the children in the district's outlying areas are now bussed to the two town schools.

First M.E. Church
Darrington, Wash. W.W.W

*Darrington's first church was the Methodist-Episcopal Church built in 1906.
It was located on the north side of town, north of the present Seeman Street
and east of Sauk Avenue. Photo by and courtesy of W. Ward Woodward.*

Chapter 7

Religion Comes To Town

The first ten or fifteen years of life in Darrington proceeded without the benefit of any church or organized religious services. The single, adventuring men who were probing the mountains for material fortune probably felt little need to satisfy their souls. However, as the community grew and more families moved in, there was a need felt for religious experience and the fellowship a church could provide. There was a special concern that children in the community would have a religious education.

Consequently, about 1904 a Sunday school was organized in the school house under the leadership of A. B. "Grandpa" Towne, a supply pastor with the Methodist-Episcopal denomination. With Towne's inspiration, a local Methodist-Episcopal Church was founded in 1906. A year later Methodist Conference records listed sixteen members of the Darrington congregation. They paid their pastor $200 a year plus $24 in expenses. [1]

Very few details about Towne's life are remembered. His granddaughter, Pearl Towne Reece, said he was born in Michigan or Minnesota. He was a Union Soldier during the Civil War. He came to the Northwest in 1900 and to Darrington in about 1902. Whether he was trained as a pastor or not isn't known, but Mrs. Reece said Darrington was his only pastorate. Grandpa Towne served as pastor until 1913 and died in April 1914. Grandma Towne, who worked alongside her husband in the ministry, died in 1926.

The congregation built a church in 1906 on the north side of town, north of the present Seeman Street and east of Sauk Avenue. Grandpa Towne, Charles Burns, the prospector-businessman who figured so brightly in Darrington's mining era, plus one other man whose name is not recorded did most of the construction work on the church building. The church's first parsonage was built in 1914-15 next door to the church. It was torn down in 1974. The church was moved to its present location in 1938. A new building with a separate bell tower housing the original church bell was built in the 1960's.

During the early years the church sponsored a youth group called the Epworth League, held regular Sunday School classes, had an active Ladies Aid Society and held morning and evening services on Sunday. The teacher, N. C. Rhoads, organized the first youth group. In the late 1920's the church started the first Boy Scout troop in town with the Rev. Paul Campbell as organizer. The Scouts met in the old schoolhouse where Sunday school had begun in 1904.

In 1918 Roy M. Owen, a bachelor, and his mother, Emma Gene Owen, moved into the Methodist parsonage just in time for the flu epidemic of that year. He and his mother were remembered in later years for their care of the sick during that epidemic.

Owen did not confine his ministry to Darrington during the years he served there. He was a "sky pilot," a traveling pastor who made the rounds of logging camps and outlying communities.[2] In the camps — Sound, Danneher and Washington Spar — he didn't do much preaching. Mainly he showed slides, using a gas-light projector, and brought magazines and newspapers for the men to read. His reception varied from camp to camp. He found the Sound camp welcomed him most. At Danneher's camp he felt his way cautiously: "It was a rough place," he recalled in later years. In the camps he felt his job was mainly to entertain and to bring a little time of socializing and fellowship to the hard-working men. However, he did hold a preaching service at Hazel once a week where the community people had formed a Sunday School, and he occasionally held services in the school house on Sauk Prairie.

Monday mornings he started out with his pack of clothes, newspapers, magazines, slides and projector. He'd ride to Hazel on a handcar with the railroad crew. Sometimes he'd pitch in and help them put in a tie, repair a track or build a culvert. Then at 10 a.m. he'd begin his house calls. He'd hold a preaching service and then in the evening would flag down the train of empties returning to Darrington and catch a ride to the Sound camp on the Prairie. Tuesday through Friday he'd make the rounds of the camps on foot and visit scattered families along the way. On the weekend he'd return to town to hold services at the local church.

Between 1929 and 1944 the Darrington church shared a pastor with the Arlington Church as it does now. However in 1944 the Ladies Aid Society and the church board were determined to get a resident pastor. A new parsonage was needed in order to provide a decent home for the prospective pastor's family. In the church history compiled by Flora McCulloch Howe in 1956, she wrote about the "new" parsonage:

> Mrs. Forbes and Mrs. Hilton Sr. were appointed to order a bunk house. They hiked up to the Spar where the bunk houses were on display and ordered the best looking of the lot. Nevertheless, they were severely critized when the dilapidated bunk house arrived. Mrs. Bennett, wife of Rev. Bennett who was to be our next pastor, came up to see what her new home was like. Later she told the ladies that she just didn't know how she could possibly live in that shack. But the women had a surprise in store for Mrs. Bennett. They went to work with a will. They papered, they painted. Esther Towne and Mrs. Sterling were in on this. Mrs. Hilton and Mrs. Tathum laid most of the linoleum. Mrs. Hilton and Tom Long finished the back porch the day before the Bennetts arrived. Mrs. Bennett made the women feel she appreciated very much what had been done.

In the 1940's the church flourished, supported primarily by an active group of young people. Music was their forte and the choir, often accompanied by a number of musicians, brought new life to worship services and provided many special musical programs.

By 1949, church attendance had dwindled to a "scattering few." Collections were small. A woman pastor, Nellie Cook, was assigned to the church by the conference. She volunteered to live in the church basement so that the parsonage could be rented out for $35 a month. Aggravated by life in the damp basement, rheumatism soon became such a problem for the pastor that she had to leave before the year was out.

In the 1960's the church in Darrington again began sharing a pastor with the Arlington Church. For a while the parsonage was rented out, but later it was razed.

Throughout the church's history, women have played a predominant role, first through the Ladies Aid Society and later through the Women's Society for Christian Service. Fund raising for church projects and service to the community have been constant goals of the women of the church since the first decade of the century.

For years the Methodist Church was the only church in the community, and its members and attenders came from many denominational backgrounds. However, with a growing number of Southerners in the area, it was almost inevitable that a Baptist Church would be formed, and it was. It took root out on Sauk Prairie where families gathered for Sunday School in various school houses or for prayer meetings in their homes for many years before a church was formed. [3]

Sunday School and prayer meetings weren't enough for the Baptist people, however. They prevailed upon different men to "preach" for them for varying periods of time, sometimes regularly, sometimes now and then. Brother L. J. Smith, a sawmill operator, at first preached occasionally, but in the months prior to the actual formation of the church he preached regularly. The Rev. J.S. Sitten and W.H. White conducted evangelistic meetings. Luther Ramey, "at the request of the community," supplied a sermon once a month for a year until his death. Some of these men were what the Carolina people called "jack-leg preachers" — unlicensed, unordained laymen feeling the call to preach.

The actual formation of the Sauk Valley Baptist Church, which later would become the First Baptist Church of Darrington, took place on July 24, 1921. T.E. Long, church clerk, recorded those historic proceedings in the church record book:

> Sunday, July 24, 1921, was a day of rejoicing for the Baptist saints in Sauk Valley, Washington.
> On Thursday evening preceding, Rev. John E. Kanarr, District Missionary, preached a cheerful sermon on Gospel Blessings. On Friday afternoon, Rev. Earl Cochran, of Lyman, led in a Baptismal service at the riverside. Where he immersed Messers. S.M. Bates and John Atkins, who were

converted in Gospel meetings held recently by Kanarr and Cochran. And on Friday and Saturday evenings, Rev. J.F. Watson, D.D., Superintendent of State Missions, preached two practical and helpful sermons.

On Sunday morning Dr. Watson gave an appropriate and soulful message, and then led the Baptist people in effecting a temporary Church organization.

Since these were all-day services the good women prepared a basket dinner and the large congregation fared sumptuously during the noon hour. In the afternoon Dr. Watson gave us another timely message and led in completing the church organization.[4]

The fledgling congregation did not stop at church organization that day. It also voted to build a church near the Skagit-Snohomish County line. The church building would be thirty by fifty-six feet, with sixteen feet partitioned off the rear to make two rooms. The congregation voted to apply to the Western Washington Baptist Convention for an appropriation of up to $88 on a basis of four dollars from the convention for every dollar from the community.

Charter members of the Sauk Valley Baptist Church were Mr. and Mrs. M. C. Forrister, Mr. and Mrs. T. E. Long, Mr. and Mrs. Sam Bates, Mr. and Mrs. J. P. Crawford, Mr. A. B. Crawford, Mrs. Lavina Wright, Mrs. Estella Herman, Mr. John Atkins, Mrs. Avery Bryson and Mr. and Mrs. L.J. Smith.

The church building, constructed on an acre of land donated by J. P. Crawford, was completed by the spring of 1922 despite the fact that the shingles for the roof had to be thawed out before they were put on.

Until August 1922 the church had no official pastor. Even the acting pastor had moved to Sedro-Woolley, leaving the new congregation pastor-less. In August, however, the church agreed to unite with the Concrete Baptist Church in hiring a pastor who would divide his time between two congregations. The pastor was John E. Kanarr, district missionary for the Western Washington Baptist Convention. Sauk Valley Church's share in his salary was $33.33 a month.

Hardly a month went by in those early days without one or two people joining the congregation either by confession of faith and baptism or by letter from another church. In this way the church slowly and steadily grew.

Then in May 1930 Harve J. Stanberry of North Carolina, an evangelist and relative of Dave Mallonee, superintendent of Sauk River Lumber Co., came to town. He was asked to preach at the Sauk Valley Church. According to T. E. Long, he preached on Mother's Day, and by the end of the sermon there wasn't a dry eye in the church. Stanberry was asked to conduct evangelistic services, but the congregation wanted to meet in Darrington where more people could be reached. Mallonee volunteered to clean up Stohr's old barn in town for the revival services. Lumber was ordered from the Fortson mill to build rough benches and a platform and pulpit. Mallonee put a crew of his men to work to build the needed furniture.

The evangelistic services continued for a week. Then again in August, Stanberry conducted two more weeks of revival. Many people made a profession of faith in Jesus Christ. At the end of the services fifty-three people were brought into the church by letter or by baptism. The baptismal service for nineteen people was held at Squire Creek.

Now, with many newly baptized believers in Darrington itself, there was talk of starting a Baptist Church within the town. Dr. Watson, still serving as executive secretary of the state convention, advised against the formation of a second Baptist church in such close proximity to the Sauk Valley Church. At his suggestion a committee was founded "to investigate and decide where was the proper place for church, in Darrington or at the present site." The congregation voted to accept the Cole Ensley site in Darrington.

On September 1, a building committee was appointed, and the congregation voted to change its name from Sauk Valley Baptist Church to First Baptist Church of Darrington. September 2 work began on the new building. On November 23, 1930, the first service was held in the new building.

In the 1930's the first mention of a church parsonage is made in the minutes, and the burden of making payments on a house and paying insurance on it was added to the burden of paying for a new church building.

In 1948 the congregation began to discuss the possibility of adding eight classrooms to the existing church building. A building fund was set up, but the matter of adding to the church was set aside until 1952 when the building fund was reactivated. In 1954 serious planning was begun for a church addition. An architect was hired in December of that year. Not only would a

Christian education wing be added but a baptistry and dressing rooms would be part of the plans as well as refurbishing of the sanctuary. In November 1956 the new building was dedicated. Later new flooring and pews and carpeting were added to the sanctuary.

Through the years the church has served the community in various ways. Besides Sunday School, it has sponsored and supported youth groups, Boy Scout and Cub Scout groups, a Temperance Association, vacation Bible schools, youth camping programs and world mission work. In 1925 it even took the dubious liberty of hosting a statewide meeting of the Knights of the Ku Klux Klan!

Another church with a long history in Darrington is the Roman Catholic Church.[5] Several of the homesteading families in the Whitehorse area were Roman Catholic. The first recorded baptism of a family member in the Darrington area was of Marie Dorina Chenier. She was baptized at Arlington on August 25, 1895. First Mass in the area was said by Father T.F. Van de Walle in 1914 at the home of John L. Campbell at Whitehorse. For many years thereafter the Campbell home served as the church for the itinerant priest and the communicants who lived in the Whitehorse area. Around 1915 Mass was said in the Joseph Chenier and Joseph Corbeil homes and in the Leland and Pioneer Hotels in town.

The history of the Roman Catholic influence in the area predates the white settlers however. Years earlier Sauk-Suiattle Indians had been contacted by priests from Omak (Squant), east of the mountains. Some, like Sauk-Suiattle leader William Moses, were given a Catholic education at St. Mary's Mission there. In 1914 Father DeRouge, S.J., made the rounds of the territory baptizing Indians and rectifying Indian marriages, but there was little follow up by later priests, according to Father Edward C. Boyle, priest in Darrington from 1958-1968.

Father Boyle recalled some of the Indian funerals he conducted, including that of William Moses. Because many of the Catholic-baptized Indians also were participants in the Shaker sect, Father Boyle knew that when he left a home after saying Rosary the night before the funeral, a Shaker service would follow his departure. Because Indian people came from far and near for the funerals, there was not enough room in the little Darrington church for everyone. The priest, coffin and the women came inside the church; the men waited outside. At the

Nine-Mile Cemetery on the Suiattle, where all the Indian burials at which he officiated took place, there was a series of speeches by the elders of the group, lamenting the death. The speeches were given in an Indian dialect but were graciously translated into English for the benefit of Father Boyle and the white undertaker. After the funerals, everyone went to the home of one of the Indians for a funeral potlatch. Father Boyle recalled that the potlatch for William Moses at Jimmy Price's ranch on the Suiattle was "magnificent" with barbecued salmon supplied abundantly.

It was the Catholic women in Darrington who put out the effort to have a church building and to provide for the visiting priests. A Catholic Women's Club was begun in September 1934 with many prominent Darrington names on the roster. Membership included Mesdames Harold Engles, J. Welch, J. Strom, Richey, Osborn, E. Boivin, Corbeil, J. Kellar, McDowell, Cunningham, Henry Keenan, B. Hansen, E. Rankin, J. L. Campbell and J. Faucett.

It was the women who provided $25 to buy six tax title lots in 1938. In 1941 they purchased a bunk house from Sauk River Lumber Co. for $300. It was transformed into a church largely through the efforts of Henry Keenan. Mrs. Mary Kellar purchased the church's first altar as a memorial to her husband. The ladies paid freight on it from San Francisco. In 1962 a second bunk house was added to the church for additional room and for religious education classes. The church is at the corner of Commercial Avenue and Riddle Street.

Monthly visits by the priest from Marysville began in 1938 and continued until about 1947 when a regularly assigned priest from Immaculate Conception Church in Arlington came weekly for Mass.

The Catholics in Darrington have been under several jurisdictions during their history. Until 1917 they were served by the priest from St. Michael's Church in Snohomish and all baptismal, marriage and funeral records from that era are in that church's records. From 1917 to 1933 Darrington Catholics were under the jurisdiction of Immaculate Conception Church, Arlington. From 1933-1947, St. Mary's Church in Marysville was the parent church. In 1947 the Darrington Church again became a mission church of Immaculate Conception Church in Arlington and remains so to the present.

The name of the church was often confusing in the early

days. Some called it St. John's; others called it St. Mary's. Archbishop Connally tried to end the confusion by officially designating it St. John Mary Vianney in honor of the Cure D'Ars, patron of Diocesan priests.

It took Darrington thirty years to establish three churches within its boundaries. In the next three decades six more churches would spring to life in the community. To an observer coming from outside, it is as if the independent and competitive spirit that marked the town's pioneers had been perpetuated in their religious life. Consequently there has never been a religious consensus in Darrington, and at this writing seven churches survive with varying degrees of attendance in a town of 1,058.

In the mid-1930's a group of people began meeting in private homes for prayer meetings and Bible study. This group would become the nucleus for the first Pentecostal church in the town and the seed group for three separate Pentecostal churches, two of which still exist.[6]

As the group grew, it met for a time in the club rooms behind the Minit Market. Sometime between 1937 and 1939 the group organized as part of the Calvary Pentecostal Church, a group of churches that had grown up in the Northwest and many of which were later absorbed by the Assembly of God. In 1941 or 1942 the congregation built a house for a church at the corner of what is now Fir Street and Sauk Avenue. In 1947 they began to construct a church building on Sauk Avenue which stood until a fire destroyed it in December 1972. A bunk house parsonage was moved to the lot adjacent to the church.

The Rev. and Mrs. Frank Funderburk were the first pastors of the new church. They were followed by the Rev. and Mrs. Carl Posey and then by the Rev. and Mrs. C. B. Andrews in 1948. The Andrews came to Darrington from Olympia where they had pastored for two or three years. Mrs. Andrews thought she had come to the end of the world when she arrived in the wooded and isolated town. The church thrived under the Andrews' leadership. An active youth group pulsed life into the congregation. The young people kept everyone informed of church happenings in a regularly issued four-page newspaper dittoed on a machine they bought with strawberry-picking money. During the height of the church's life about 100 attended Sunday school regularly.

Calvary Pentecostal Church existed until about 1960. Soon afterward its church building was sold to Grace Baptist Church.

By then its membership had dwindled to just a few families. Others had been attracted away to the newly formed Church of God of Prophecy and to the Assembly of God.

Both the Church of God of Prophecy and the Glad Tidings Assembly of God continue today. The Church of God of Prophecy remains a small congregation meeting in a church building at the corner of Sauk Avenue and Cascade Street. The Assembly of God, however, is a thriving Pentecostal Church displaying much of the enthusiasm and activity that marked its parent body, Calvary Pentecostal Church.

The Assembly was formed in 1953 by the Rev. Dwight McGlaughlin, then Northwest district superintendent of the Assemblies of God, with the assistance of the Rev. Maynard Oss, pastor of the Arlington Assembly of God Church. The early church meetings were held in the home of Raymond Green on Sauk Prairie. The first pastor was the Rev. Clyde Husan.

In the fall of 1953, Ike Green, Floyd Spence, Dave Estes and Andrew Peterson went together to purchase land west of Darrington on Highway 530 in order to build a church. The church was completed in the late spring of 1954. The parsonage next door was completed shortly afterward.

Rev. Husan completed his ministry in Darrington in the spring of 1955, and the church's second pastor, the Rev. Henry D. Bridgman, was called to the pastorate there in April. During Bridgman's ministry the church saw its greatest growth, averaging 130 at services in 1961. It also suffered its greatest disappointment as the local plywood mill closed its doors and several active families were forced to move elsewhere to seek employment.

During Bridgman's ministry a kitchen and a fellowship hall were built on the north side of the church and the parsonage was expanded. While Bridgman pastored the congregation, several people in the church began a well-attended and still-continuing outreach to the community, a midweek children's Bible club. The Bible club is often attended by seventy-five to 100 children, many of whom attend other churches regularly on Sundays.

Not only did the Pentecostal churches proliferate in Darrington as unresolved differences in opinion surfaced in the congregations, but disagreements at the First Baptist Church led to the formation of two other Baptist churches as well. Mountain View Baptist Church [7] was organized in 1954 by Rev. William Breedlove, a former pastor of the First Baptist Church, and aligned itself with the Southern Baptist Convention. (First Baptist is affiliated with the American Baptist Convention). Frank Brooks of North Carolina was called to be the church's first pastor, serving the congregation as it met in an old Washington Veneer Co. bunkhouse at Bennettville and later in what was called "the old Indian house" on Emens Street in Darrington. Later a church building was constructed on Fullerton Avenue.

Charter members of the church were Ted Buchanan, on whose property the church-bunkhouse was located, J. P. Crawford, James McMahan, Ida McMahan, Bill Christopher, Florence Christopher, David Green, Margaret Green, Carl Jones, Bonnie Green, Mildred Green, Bragg Parris, Frank Brooks and Eula Brooks.

Grace Baptist Church originated in 1961 after internal friction at First Baptist Church led to a split of opinion in the congregation and the departure of several families. The church was aligned with the Conservative Baptist Convention. The small congregation met in a bunk house on the church property on Sauk Avenue after its church building burned in 1972. It has disbanded since that time.

In 1956 Episcopalians in Darrington met together for the first time to worship at the Community Center.[8] Seventeen attended the first service, called together by a notice in the *Timber Bowl Tribune*, the local newspaper. The notice was placed by Archdeacon Walter W. McNeil, Jr., who served the mission churches of the Diocese of Olympia. People involved in the founding of the local congregation were Mr. and Mrs. Harry Van Arnum and family, Miss Mae Phillips, Mrs. Bess Shattuck, the Dearinger family, Miss Alice Elinor Lambert, Mr. and Mrs. Leonard Hall and family and Mr. and Mrs. Chuck Neideigh. Shortly after the people began to meet regularly for worship they sought a church to meet in. The Methodists gave them the use of their building on Sunday evenings. Shortly afterwards the Diocese bought land across from the Catholic Church, and a bunk house was purchased and moved to the site. Archdeacon McNeil remembers the bunk house well. He recalled in a letter written in 1975:

> Just after the move, I left on a month's holiday, and when I last saw the bunkhouse it was sort of teetering at an angle. Shortly after I returned, Bishop (Rt. Rev. Stephen) Bayne was due at Darrington to dedicate the new church,

so I called the senior warden, Mr. Van Arnum, and asked him how they were coming with the renovation. His answer was, 'Well, we have had an awfully busy summer and haven't gotten around to doing anything.' You can imagine how my heart fell when I heard this, so I decided to travel up there and take a look. When I rounded the corner, I saw this beautiful church, all renovated, freshly painted, and a crew working on the last details of renovation. They were keeping from the Archdeacon the fact that the church was going to be ready for the dedication. I offered praises to God when I saw the beauty of that building.

The Episcopal Church in Darrington owes its name to Archdeacon McNeil. Early in his ministry he had served a beautiful little church in Moose, Wyoming, which was called Church of the Transfiguration. A plate glass window in the church looked out over the Grand Tetons. McNeil loved that little church and suggested that the Darrington church also carry the name. The people agreed.

The first priest to be assigned regularly to the church was the Rev. Wesley Frensdorf who came in 1958. He and his family lived in Darrington, and he served the Darrington church and congregations in Newhalem and Rockport for three and a half years.

Chapter 8

Doing Business

From its inception, Darrington was a community torn in two directions. Should it be related primarily to Arlington down the Stillaguamish Valley? Or should its trade relationships be with communities on the Skagit? The railroads had competed for Darrington's promising mining business, one proposing a route up the Sauk from the Skagit; the other proposing — and building a railroad up the Stillaguamish. Even with the railroad tugging it in the direction of other Snohomish County communities, Darrington continued to lean toward Skagit settlements already connected to it by a wagon road. Enterprising Darrington people played their tune both ways, urging both Snohomish and Skagit counties to come through with road and bridge money. Slowly — too slowly at times for Darrington businessmen and miners — the primary tie with Arlington and Snohomish County was forged while the Sauk-Skagit route diminished to secondary importance.

A passable wagon road from communities on the Skagit to Darrington was already in use in the 1890's. Three bicyclists used that road one July day in 1897 to travel from Hamilton to Darrington. The Darrington correspondent reported that the gentleman and his two lady companions "wanted to go on to Arlington but could not on account of poor roads, consequently they returned the way they came over a good road that can be traveled at all seasons. If Arlington desires to retain the trade of this section she will have to make a howl at headquarters for bridge money. The mines and others will complete the road so a team can get over it.'"[1]

So began a campaign to build a usable freight road up the Stillaguamish. In 1899 H. G. Price brought the first wagon freight up that route, but by no means was the road in shape for constant use. It could hardly be called a road. Darrington people complained that the county commissioners were not taking adequate steps to build and maintain a good road. For a long time the future Arlington-Darrington road stopped at Oso. Then at Hazel after a gap of ten miles, the North Fork Road, as it was called, continued up the valley to town. In between Oso and Hazel there was a trail. Despite that problem, two adventurous businessmen, Messrs. Galbraith and Bacon of Seattle brought the first car up to Darrington in August 1907.

By the fall of 1910 most of the initial work on a primitive single lane road through the woods and The Burn, as the area between Arlington and Darrington was called, had been completed. Bridges still needed to be built, however, over many streams. French Creek was the last creek to be spanned in 1912.

By 1914 a few hardy autoists were venturing up the slightly improved road to Darrington and continuing on to Hamilton and Concrete on the Skagit. Snohomish County Road Superintendent Frank Connors was the second driver to make the day-long excursion. He recommended that the drive be made in dry weather and that autoists should take along a rope in case they got stuck on the sand hills.[2]

On August 27, 1915, a group of fifty people from Arlington traveled for three or three and a half hours in eight autos from Arlington to Darrington. There they were hosted by a group of Darrington residents. One of those who took the trip wrote:

> The presence in Darrington of the eight cars, which carried about 50 people, was a convincing reminder that pioneer conditions, the day of the canoe and the pack strap has passed away, that the mere fact that a place is so many miles from some other and larger center is no reason why it should be considered in the back woods, so long as it is connected with the outside world by a road passable for that modern marvel of transportation, the automobile, for when good roads and the gasoline engine can be linked together, isolation is annihilated.[3]

During the summer of 1915, the auto department of the *Seattle Post-Intelligencer* featured an article on an auto trip to

Darrington. The writer was bowled over by Whitehorse Mountain and asked incredulously, "How have picture postcard vendors missed this mountain peak so long?" Impressed with the setting, the writer predicted that a large summer resort would be built at the base of Whitehorse.[4]

From that year on, auto sightseers have been making the trip to Darrington and exclaiming over the town's magnificent setting. However, no one has ever built a resort near Darrington.

Darrington's evolution from a prospector's boom town accessible only by foot or canoe to a settled community served by a railroad and improving roads was rapid. Only eleven years passed between the arrival of the first settler by canoe and the arrival of the first train. Ten more years and the automobile had begun its invasion into the life of the mountain community.

Even though Darrington had its road by 1915, it would be a long time before it would be paved from end to end. Dr. N. C. Riddle, who came to Darrington in 1929, told a newspaper reporter once that the road was so dusty in the summer you couldn't see and so rutted in the winter you were never sure of making it. Most of the time it was easier to stay home, "for when you started out of Darrington, you wished you hadn't."[5]

Darrington's relationship with its own "out back", the Sauk Prairie, was not permanently cemented until a bridge was built across the Sauk near Darrington in 1930, connecting with a wagon road that wound its way through the Forest Reserve and out to Mansford on the Prairie, about eight or ten miles from town. In 1921 or '22 a ferry had been put in service at what was called Kahoots Crossing north of the present bridge. At that time Snohomish and Skagit counties had cooperated to slightly improve the Prairie road which followed an old Sound Timber Co. railroad right of way.

Before the Kahoots crossing ferry was put into service, Sauk Prairie residents tended to take their trade to Skagit communities since a ferry had been in service connecting the north end of the Prairie with Bennettville since before 1897. The original ferry line was washed out in 1897 and was rebuilt a little farther downriver.

Both the ferries across the Sauk proved undependable, however, leaving Sauk Prairie residents without connections to the outside world whenever there was high water. (A foot bridge at Darrington, the only other connection between the Prairie and town, was washed out prior to 1921 and never was rebuilt.) Arlington and Darrington businessmen argued that an auto bridge would be a money-saver since the ferry operator received $75 a month from the county. Once again Arlington-Darrington businessmen vied with Skagit County counterparts for the business and trade of the agricultural Prairie. Skagit was building roads and bridges that soon would connect Darrington's hinterlands with trade centers on the Skagit. Time was running out.

Forest Service Ranger J. R. Bruckhart was one of the early supporters of the bridge. His successor, Harold Engles, also supported bridge construction and convinced the U.S. government to include $5,000 in the district's 1929 budget to help prime the Snohomish County pump for a bridge. He argued that a bridge would benefit the Forest Service, giving it quicker access to the east side of the river to fight fires.

After many false starts, the bridge was constructed and opened in October 1930 with a town celebration which was attended by 600 people. The new bridge served thirty-three families living on 3,000 acres of cultivated land. The span cost $38,000.

Before the railroad came to Darrington in 1901, the town was little more than a place where prospectors could get supplies and liquor. Lawrence "Toby" Freese recalled that maybe there were twenty-five or thirty people living within what are now the town limits when he arrived in March 1901 as a five-year-old.

The one store was Montague and Moore's. There were about six houses, if he recalled correctly, and three taverns, one being a tent tavern. There were three dug wells in town when he and his family arrived by pack train from Sauk City at the confluence of the Sauk and Skagit Rivers. The family had come from Wisconsin the year before and stayed in Snohomish for the winter. They took the railroad from Snohomish via Arlington to Sauk City on the Skagit where they transferred their belongings to the pack train. They could have come up the wagon road that followed the Stillaguamish, but the Sauk City route was ten miles shorter.

Toby's parents were barbers, so his stepfather put up a tent shelter at what is now the south end of Montague Avenue to

The new Moore store is pictured sometime between 1909 and 1916 when it burned down. The Darrington Post Office is at the right. Note the wooden sidewalk with railings. Photo by and courtesy of W. Ward Woodward.

serve both as a home and barbershop. He made a barber chair out of cedar, tacked up a sign, and waited for business.

The first customer was a hairy prospector who needed a haircut. Fred Freese cut the man's hair and charged him the going rate of "two bits." Mrs. Freese put out her hand for the money; she needed to buy supplies at Montague and Moore's. But Freese said no, that was the first money he had earned in this town and he intended to keep it as a souvenir. With that he hammered the money to one of the tent poles.

Before winter the elder Freese had built a split cedar cabin for his family on the site where the family later built a boarding house. Until recently Toby Freese and his wife lived in part of the old boarding house that was built before 1908.

One of the first business establishments of any permanence in Darrington was Montague and Moore's Trading Post. John Montague had lived on the Stillaguamish River since 1888, working in logging camps in the lowlands around Florence and later filing a homestead claim at Oso. In 1899 he moved to Darrington where he bought a block of property on which to build a general merchandise store.

About 1900 Charles E. Moore, who had also settled near Oso in 1891 and who had run a general store-hotel-post office there with a man by the name of Carroll, moved to Darrington to go into partnership with Montague. In 1905 the store did $20,000 worth of business, no small sum for that year and the isolated location of the town.

In 1907 Moore's nephew, W. Ward Woodward,[6] arrived from Michigan with his bride of eleven days to help in the store. Montague had died in March of that year, and Moore was running the establishment alone.

The "establishment" was a little cluster of buildings east of the railroad tracks and south of what is now Darrington Street where it turns to go toward Clear Creek. A barn, warehouse, butcher shop and the log cabin store made up the "shopping center." According to Woodward, it carried "everything from soup to nuts."

Rooms above the warehouse housed traveling salesmen — "drummers" — who plied their wares by train. For a time the warehouse rooms were the living quarters for Edith and Ward Woodward. Woodward recalled that the bedbugs were terrible.

In 1909 Moore built a big, trim two-story building to house his growing stock. That building was constructed behind the earlier buildings which were left standing. The new building faced toward the west and the growing cluster of structures that now began to form the town center. Beside the store was the little post office where Moore served as postmaster.

By 1910 there were two good-sized hotels in town, The Leland and The Pioneer, plus Freese's boarding house, the Kennet brothers hotel on Montague Avenue and one other lodging house. There was a train depot. A little building on the main street housed a barber shop. Tom Dorgan had opened a meat market. A second general merchandise store, known for years as The Darrington Store, was located on the main street. Near the railroad tracks north of town center was Sam Furland's livery stable and blacksmith shop. From a vantage point near Moore's new store about fifteen houses could be spotted scattered among the stumps of the newly logged townsite west of the railroad tracks and north of what is now Darrington Street. Altogether there were sixty buildings in the community according to the 1910 census. The population was 250 and for some reason it was noted that there were fourteen pianos in town. [7]

Just three years before, the town had been suffering from its first housing shortage as the population expanded from twenty-five or thirty in 1901 to 250 in 1910. The little place was booming with the hope of minerals in the hills.

The new Moore store burned down August 17, 1916, and Charles Moore, tired of keeping store, married his cook-chambermaid-post office helper and moved to Virginia.

Woodward then went to work for Charles Runkel, the owner of the Darrington Store. In 1917 Woodward decided to become a proprietor himself, and made the first payment toward the purchase of the store. In the same year Woodward made another move. He applied for the position of postmaster, a position he held until December 31, 1955. "When I got to be seventy years old, I had to quit," he said years later.

Woodward often did extra duty as town postmaster and storekeeper. One year the railroad tracks washed out at Cicero, just east of Arlington. Every day Woodward would take a handcar down to the washout to meet someone from Arlington who had pumped up to the washout with the mail. They would exchange mail, and Woodward would pump himself back to town, a distance of over twenty miles.

After the washout was repaired, a center pier on the railroad bridge at Cicero went out. The tracks were still connected, but they sagged dangerously. No trains could run across the bridge, and repairs were slow.

It was Thanksgiving time, and Woodward wanted his store patrons to have their traditional Thanksgiving dinners. He and Bob Bothell took it upon themselves to pump the handcar all the way to Arlington and back, loaded with turkeys, oysters and all the dinner trimmings on the return trip.

It took them a day and a half of pumping, shopping and pumping home to do their errand. At the Cicero bridge they had to fasten a line to the handcar and pull it across after them rather than risk riding it across the sagging tracks. But Thanksgiving turkeys and oysters made it to town.

Asked to describe the town to which he and his wife had come in 1907, Woodward smiled and said, "Wild and wooley." The population was on its way to 250, he recollected, and by that time the number of taverns had grown to seven. By that time, too, there was a "red light district," in fact two houses of ill repute.

But Ward Woodward said that despite the free use of liquor in the town, "We've had some good times. We had some good dances over the old bowling alley. Even with all the liquor around we had a nice clean dance." The bowling alley he referred to was built on the corner of Elwell Avenue and Darrington Street. Downstairs was the bowling alley and tavern. Upstairs was a hall that doubled as dance hall and later as a movie house.

The two major hotels in town were both started by Joseph Chenier around the turn of the century. Chenier, a Canadian, had moved to the Stillaguamish Valley in 1890 or 1893, living on a homestead near Fortson. Both of his hotels, The Pioneer and The Leland were close to the railroad depot. Though Chenier owned both hotels, the Hotel Leland was operated for him by Mr. and Mrs. Joseph Corbeil. John Knudson had built a hotel on Commercial Street in anticipation of the new railroad line passing that way, but he had misjudged, and his building was left standing useless at an inconvenient distance from the depot. The second floor of the intended hotel was later converted to a photography studio for himself.

The Pioneer Hotel was owned and operated for years by Henry Keenan who married one of Joe Chenier's daughters. Keenan and his brothers came from Ontario, Canada, to the Darrington area in 1900 to cut shingle bolts and ties for the railroad. For a time the Keenan boys operated one of the several saloons in town.

Charles E. Moore, general store proprietor, 1900-1916. Photo by and courtesy of W. Ward Woodward.

In 1902 Henry Keenan and Permelia Chenier were married, and in 1907 Keenan took his family to Canada where they stayed for ten years. In 1918, after his return from Canada, Keenan took over the operation of the Pioneer Hotel from his father-in-law.

Keenan ran a good hotel. He didn't allow drinking or any carousing on the premises. He demanded absolute quiet after 10 p.m. in deference to lodgers who had to get up early to work in the woods. If necessary he would use force to throw out any lodgers or loiterers who failed to follow the house rules. Keenan's son-in-law, Harold Engles, said he wished there had been a swinging door on the hotel lobby, because Keenan often broke the door off its hinges in his haste to get rid of a troublemaker.

Keenan was known as "The Law" in town long before there were official lawmen, and even *after* there were some official ones. He was often the one called on by frightened residents to break up fights or to cool threatening ones.

The story is told about a constant troublemaker who showed up one morning at one of the town's eating places, brandishing a knife and balancing a head full of liquor. He held everyone in the room at bay by sauntering about, flipping the knife indiscriminately into the air, and waving it uncomfortably close to customers' ears and noses. The sheriff was called, but he took one look at the situation and decided he couldn't handle it. He called Keenan who told him, "If you'll deputize me for the next half hour, I'll take care of that character. He's been asking for it too long." Keenan then walked into the room where the man still had charge and with one well-aimed fist, ended the trouble for the day.[8]

Keenan operated the Pioneer Hotel until 1944 when it was sold to a man from Seattle. In 1948 the hotel changed hands again and was operated by the Anacortes Veneer Co. as a lodging place for its men and headquarters for its logging works. Later Ace Comstock moved into the hotel with his family and for a short time ran a weekly newspaper there. In February 1969 the old abandoned hotel burned to the ground in what could have been a disastrous fire had there not been an unusually heavy snow pack on and around adjacent buildings.

In March 1917, Roy F. Wolfe,[9] a pharmacist, arrived in town from Index, Washington, to open the first pharmacy. A wholesale druggist had told Wolfe about the Darrington opportunity. Logging was opening up in the area, and the town's physician, Dr. B. T. Blake, was caring for about 2,000 loggers and mill workers on a contract basis. He needed a pharmacist.

The first pharmacy was in a two-story building at the corner of Railroad Avenue and Darrington Street, across from Hotel Leland. It contained two stores and two storerooms. Wolfe shared the building with a barber.

A few years later he moved into the Petersen Building, just a lot to the west. Wolfe set up an ice cream fountain in the spacious building in addition to his pharmacy. "I had a pretty complete

A group of unidentified fishermen pose in front of the Pioneer Hotel sometime during the 1920's. Henry Keenan, hotel keeper, is third from right. Keenan ran the hotel from 1918 to 1944. The abandoned structure burned in 1969. The car is an Oakland, about a 1923 model. Photo courtesy of W. Ward Woodward.

store," Wolfe recalled. In addition to prescription compounds he stocked many of the popular patent medicines like Pinkham's Compound and Sal Hepatica. White wrought iron chairs and tables — some of them child-size — could seat forty customers in those days. The ice cream for the fountain was kept cold by 200 pounds of ice a week brought up by train from Arlington. Sometimes the ice cream went bad, though, and Wolfe's wife, assisted by Ward Woodward's wife, would make delicious sour cream cookies out of the spoiled mixture. Wolfe's ice cream parlor was a busy place on dance and movie nights in the small town, providing an alternative meeting and refreshment place to the town's taverns.

Wolfe moved his store two times more, finally locating in a brick building which he built on Darrington Street and which was still used in 1975 to house a dress shop and a beauty shop. Shortly after it was completed, half the building was rented to the Donaldson Brothers who operated the first electric company in Darrington and who provided the town with electricity in 1926.

Wolfe recalls the hard times the town suffered after World War I. He says that starting in 1921 he "just about starved out" and didn't get back on his feet until 1926. In 1942 Wolfe sold the business to August Petersen and went into semi-retirement on his farm outside of Darrington which he had purchased in 1932.

While the good times lasted — and after they were restored — the town was really lively for a small place.

Dr. Blake and Wolfe went together to build the King Tut Dance Hall between the Petersen Building and Wolfe's pharmacy building. The hall was used as a dance hall, movie house, community hall, basketball court and boxing hall for many years before it was burned down in 1951, allegedly by a fire bug of a town marshall. That fire also destroyed the old Red Top Tavern, shoe shop and barber shop and threatened the entire town when a water main burst, diminishing water pressure. The Arlington Fire Co. plus volunteers from the U. S. Forest Service, Washington State Forestry Department, Washington Veneer Co., Anacortes Veneer Co., Three Rivers Mill Co., Jones and Anderson, and Roy Loughnan aided the Darrington Fire Department in saving the town. Damage from the fire was estimated at $75,000. [10]

The town was lively during the Prohibition era since distance from law enforcement agencies and a cooperative county sheriff, so the story goes, helped the tavern business even in dry times.

Wolfe told an amusing story of an Everett Eagle Lodge gathering at the old Red Top Tavern (located across the street and west of the present Red Top). It was Prohibition times, and someone had brought a keg of moonshine which was kept in the curtained compartment of a Ford touring car. The clever supplier had a hose down in the barrel which led out through the curtains of the car. The Eagles gathered around the car taking long sips through the siphon. They danced and they drank. That night the happy group started homeward along the muddy, rutted Arlington-Darrington Road. Not far from town they got mired in the mud, and in their condition were unable to get themselves out. Some sympathetic townspeople came to their aid; but as Wolfe said, "It was an awfully *wet* bunch of Eagles!"

It was from Prohibition days that Darrington apparently got its reputation for being an especially wild and wooley place, a reputation that has been hard to shake in the ensuing years. But Wolfe claims that it was only on weekends that the town lived up to its reputation. Sunday was a day off, and loggers from the logging camps nearby came into town to celebrate their leisure. The Swedes had a favorite tavern. So did the Tarheels (the men from North Carolina). "Before the day was over, there'd always be a scrap out on the street between the two groups," Wolfe recalled. Unfortunately, Sunday was the day when sightseers from towns "down below" would venture to Darrington. "As a result, we'd get some of the darndest write-ups in the paper about the 'war' in Darrington," Wolfe said.

Though Darrington may have been a source of amusement for newspaper readers down below, the small community really went about making itself a livable town almost from the very first. It attempted an orderly development, and real estate venturers filed plat maps for the community as early as 1900. Plats were filed by Moran and Co. and Lester K. Alvord, the Knudson Brothers and Park and Johnson. By 1901 there were three forty-acre tracts and one twenty-acre tract in the townsite. Lots were thirty by 120 feet; roads were sixty feet wide, except for two which were eighty feet.[11] Although it would not be incorporated until 1945, the town made its first attempt at incorporation in 1901 with only sixteen signatures on the petition![12]

A telephone system was installed in 1907 by the Farmer's Telephone Co. The first switchboard was located in Freese's boarding house, and Toby Freese recalls doing service as substitute switchboard operator. He claims that some of his calls were from worried wives asking him to keep an eye on the plank walk between a nearby tavern and the whorehouse and to call back if he saw their husbands heading towards trouble.

For years the town depended on wells for water. However, an early water system was installed in 1904 by O. A. Seeman to provide water to homes in the Seeman and Randall additions of town. A well, gasoline pump, 165-barrel tank and 2,600 feet of four-and-a-half-inch stave pipe provided water to the homes. Elsewhere families shared wells which were scattered about the town.[13]

In 1919 Stillman Frost began installing a water system, which, with considerable updating, still serves the town. However, some of the original cedar water mains still serviced homes along Montague Avenue as late as 1974. Still Frost willed it to Frank Frost. After Frank's death his widow sold the water system to Charles Six. Toby Freese bought the system in 1948. The town finally bought the water system in September 1977.

Electric power came to Darrington in 1926 when Troz and Barney Donaldson installed an electric line from Oso to Darrington. Cost at first was a whopping 14 cents per kilowatt hour. Many homes had one light bulb — seldom used, but a symbol of progress and civilization. The Donaldsons later sold their system to Puget Sound Light Co. For years electric power was undependable in Darrington. (Out on the Sauk Prairie there was no electric power until the 1950's.) Many people held out against buying electric ranges because of the guarantee of interrupted service. One of the families who resisted electric cooking was the Dr. N.C. Riddle family. Troz Donaldson tried to talk the Riddles into an electric stove, but they clung to the wood stove and wood heater. One year the two families planned to share Christmas dinner at the Donaldson's. Of course it would be cooked electrically. Christmas Eve there was a power disruption. Christmas morning the power was still off. Early that morning an embarrassed Donaldson arrived at the Riddle's home with an uncooked turkey tucked under his arm. Christmas dinner was prepared on the Riddle's ever-dependable wood stove.[14]

Darrington's first movie house was opened by Mrs. W. A. Gerdon in 1923. Known as the Rex Theater, it was housed in the Nels Petersen building at the corner of Railroad Avenue and Darrington Street. Movies were scheduled Wednesday and Saturday each week. The first showbill included "River's End" and the comedy, "Toonerville Trolley."[15]

Darrington got its first real jail the same year it got a movie house. In the early days a box car on a siding had served as a jail for a brief time. Then for many years there was no official lock-up for troublemakers. Some of the townspeople thought the town needed a jail. One of those who campaigned for an adequate jail was Sam Strom, the colorful miner, sharp shooter and sometime lawman. In a letter to *The Arlington Times* in July 1921, Strom complained that he knew that "a few chronic drunkards and a small petty larceny hoodlum gang by their actions seem to have decided on Darrington as a likely spot for

This view of Darrington, originally a panorama, had to be split into three sections to reproduce here. The photo, taken in about 1910, shows, from top left, Moore's store, post office, Northern Pacific tracks heading toward the Iowa Mill, Mrs. Freese's boarding house, the Pioneer Hotel, one of the town's saloons, and the Hotel Leland. Up the street from the Hotel Leland, the building with the false front is the Darrington Store, now known as the Minit Market. Of the other buildings, Freese's boarding house was the only one standing in 1978.

uninterrupted operation of bootlegging, petty larceny, and in a few instances, of serious crimes."

His letter went on: "The people of Darrington and vicinity have been imposed upon too long by this sort of night howling and shooting of firearms and petty stealing that has been carried on around here in the last few months. The plain fact is that the little gang of night-howling, night-prowling conglomeration of chronic drunks, bootleggers and petty larceny thieves operating around Darrington like a bunch of Chinese high-binders needs taking care of."

There's a question whether Strom wrote with complete candor or with a campaigner's inclination for overstatement, but he closed his letter with a plea for an adequate jail and asked others to join him in urging the county commissioners and prosecuting attorney to provide Darrington with one. "It might make Darrington a better place," Strom concluded.

By 1923 someone convinced the county commissioners that Darrington did indeed need a *real* lockup, especially since it was so far away from the county jail. The county built a small jail, which, in fact, didn't provide much security. Shortly after it was put into use, a prisoner battered his way through the wooden wall and escaped. A fellow prisoner refused to go with him, got hit on the head for his obstinacy and set up a howl for deputy marshall Keenan. [16]

As Darrington became more automobile oriented, new businesses sprang up to take care of auto needs. Standard Oil opened an auxiliary supply station for gasoline and stove oil in Darrington in 1922. Another service station operated by the Vaughan Brothers opened at about the same time. An auto stage line between Arlington and Darrington, one of several through the years, began operating in the 20's providing transportation to supplement the diminishing passenger service on the train.

One of the busiest groups in town during the community's formative years was the Darrington Improvement Club, which was a sort of Chamber of Commerce. Ward Woodward was its first president when it was formed in 1924. In 1926 it had 32

A view of Darrington taken by Ward Woodward about 1910 or '12 from the high branches of a fir tree. Right foreground is Moore's store with a corner of the Northern Pacific depot visible beyond it. Hotel Leland and Sam Furland's livery stable are the other big structures visible in the town. Courtesy of W. Ward Woodward.

Darrington

WW 112

members. The Club's purpose was "to look after Darrington's interests in every respect and see that the town stays right on the map." [17] Harold Engles [18] was volunteered as the club's president shortly after his arrival as U. S. Forest Service Ranger in 1927. He recalled with fervor and a little amusement some of the club's projects.

The club put in the first five street lights in town. As Engles said, "There weren't many streets to put lights on!" It also planted shade trees to replace the evergreens that had been cleared away to make room for the town. In 1925 it published a very attractive brochure designed to invite outdoors people to Darrington and the trails beyond. The booklet was entitled "Darrington, Where the Trails Begin." The pamphlet was illustrated with photographs by J. Boyd Ellis of Arlington and gave descriptions of campgrounds and trails in the Darrington area.

One of the club's projects was putting in the portion of Emens Street which runs from Darrington Street north to the Darrington Elementary School. Previously it had been just a path winding among the tree stumps. The club proposed to blast the stumps with dynamite. It requisitioned mattresses from the townspeople to absorb some of the shock and proceeded to plant dynamite under the stumps.

One of the powder monkeys got overly enthusiastic about the job and tied four sticks together. Engles recalled the results with amusement. "People had chickens in town then. The hens were laying. But when that dynamite went off, the blast blew hens, eggs, chicken coops — the whole works — for a couple of blocks. Very few chicks were hatched that spring in that part of town."

Probably the club's longest lasting and most far-sighted achievement was the purchase of the Squire Creek Park in a joint project with the Arlington Commercial Club. The two clubs raised $800 for the twenty acres of virgin timber which was a parcel Lamson Logging Co. considered too small to log. After clearing underbrush, building shelters and doing other improvements, the clubs deeded the park to the county. In the late 20's the Squire Creek Park stand of timber stood out against a stark landscape. Except for a few scraggly hemlocks at Boulder Creek, it was the only stand of virgin timber left on the North Fork Road. The roadside park was enlarged and refurbished by the county in 1973-74 with new shelters, restrooms, trash receptacles and tables as well as a new entrance road necessitated by the construction of a new highway bridge across the creek. The park, which is about two and a half miles from Darrington on the Arlington-Darrington road, is not only heavily used by travelers but by local people who want a cool place to picnic on some of the stifling hot summer days that settle into the valley.

It was with the support of the Darrington Improvement Club that a fire department was formed in the fall of 1925. The original department had twenty-nine members with Earl Rankin as chief and Elgin Vaughan as assistant chief. First efforts of the fire department were to raise money for 500 to 1,000 feet of hose and four pump cans to be mounted on a light truck. The next project was to build a shelter for the company's lone piece of equipment.

The Improvement Club sponsored one of Darrington's liveliest Fourth of July celebrations in 1925. An estimated 1,200 people participated in the day-long celebration featuring a variety of activities to entertain all ages. There were a greased pole climb, foot races for youngsters and adults (including a fat man's race with winners coming in in this order: Joe Bennet, Mr. Bru and Dr. B. T. Blake), bicycle and tricycle races, log-bucking contest, pony races, greased pig contest and, the event of the day, a baseball game between married and single men. (The married men won 16-11 in seven innings.) The nightcap was a fireworks display. The next year the Improvement Club bowed out of sponsoring the event. It voted instead to put money into equipment for the fledgling fire department.[19]

It may well be that the 1925 Fourth of July was the biggest and best the town ever saw and probably drew the biggest crowd of people that had ever come to town or ever would come to town before the Timber Bowl celebrations began in 1946.

Timber Bowl for many years was an annual event used to raise money for community needs and to give the town the name it deserved as a logging community. As it grew, the celebration drew thousands of people, not just from local communities but from all over the Puget Sound area. Often the queen's float was entered in other Northwest summer festivals, taking the name of Darrington and its reputation as a loggers' town far away from the formerly isolated, backwoods community.

The first Timber Bowl was held in 1946 to raise money for a new fire engine and fire fighting equipment. Seven girls competed for the Timber Bowl queen's crown by selling tickets for the event. Jackie Knowles was the winning salesgirl and was crowned queen. Princesses were Betty Bruseth, Delores York, Barbara Riddle, Marilyn Chilcote, Sara Lewis and Lois Jackson.

A week of rain preceded the first Timber Bowl weekend as it often does in June in Darrington, but the sun came out just as the parade got started on June 29. The first parade featured the high school band decked out in loggers' clothes, impressive truckloads of logs, lumber, shakes and shingles, and the newest in logging equipment. The queen's float, mounted on a 12-wheel low-boy, consisted of an eight-foot section of a Douglas fir log set amid a bower of forest moss and ferns. Upon this appropriate throne sat Darrington's first queen of the timber. The princesses perched on a springboard set into the log.

That first Timber Bowl was not a polished affair, but it was a money-raiser, bringing in more money for the fire department than anyone had ever dreamed. [20]

The Timber Bowl celebration continued with only a few years' interruptions until 1967 when community enthusiasm for the 20-year-old festival died. Now the Darrington Horse Owners' Association has taken over the last weekend of June for its annual Timber Bowl Rodeo at the rodeo grounds near Squire Creek.

Darrington, long a community, became a legal entity on September 25, 1945, when it was finally incorporated as a fourth-class city. The first officials of the incorporated town were mayor Reider Westeren; council members Orville Pearson, Walter Bates, Robert Hilton Jr., Helen Lock and Leah Reece; town clerk Edna Hilton; treasurer Ida Loughnan; town marshall Robert Hilton Sr.; city attorney Clarence Coleman of Everett; justice of the peace Tom Sharpless. Council meetings were held in the Ladies Club building until 1947 when the city hall was built. [21]

News in Darrington has always had a way of getting around. Word of mouth has been — and still is — the most depended upon (and least dependable) means of communicating there. However, throughout its history the town has had three

--->

These were gas-powered passenger cars which ran on the Darrington or North Fork Branch of the Northern Pacific starting July 17, 1910. In one year the special cars traveled 43,800 miles, making two runs daily. They made 54 stops between Arlington and Darrington, crossed 64 bridges, went through four tunnels and 48 switches. The cars apparently were used on the line for about a year and a half. Photo by Lewis. Courtesy of Harold and Anna May Engles.

RAIL ROAD CROSSING

N. P. MOTOR CAR, DARRINGTON BRANCH.

PHOTO BY LEWIS, DARRINGTON WASH.

newspapers of its own to supplement the local news carried by *The Arlington Times, The Everett Herald* and the local grape-vine.

The Wrangler was the name of a newspaper published for several years by the Darrington Literary Society. The Society was founded by N. C. Rhoads, the creative teacher who came to Darrington in 1907. After Rhoads left Darrington in 1913 the society and the paper continued for at least two years. *The Wrangler* became one of the instruments with which the town tried to tell the world about itself and its promising future.

In April 1915 an editorial in *The Wrangler* boasted:

> The future of Darrington cannot be overestimated. The most prominent mining men of the country have predicted Darrington to become one of the greatest mining camps in the world. This kind of industry gives work to thousands of men, building up great cities and turning out millionaires by the score.[22]

In another issue, *The Wrangler* editor called Darrington "a very healthy infant" and boasted that the newspaper itself "has been declared by people throughout the country as a credit to any city." After listing Darrington's many favorable features and its promising future, the editor concluded: "Darrington is the most desirable location in Snohomish County if not in the State of Washington." [23]

More than thirty years after the demise of *The Wrangler*, Darrington got its second newspaper almost by accident. Frank Lock, an unemployed teacher, tinkerer, and businessman, saw an ad in a Seattle paper for some used job printing equipment. Lock had worked in 1917-1918 in the press room of *The Bellingham Herald*, and printer's ink had gotten into his system. He bought the ancient printing equipment he saw advertised and converted a truck repair shop he had behind his house into a job printing shop. After a while, on a whim, he decided to try his hand at putting out a newspaper. The year was 1947. The paper was *The Darrington News* whose flag declared it was "just like a letter from home." In fact, the largest number of subscribers to the paper were in North Carolina, either friends or family of Darrington residents or former Darrington people.

Usually the paper had four pages. Pages one and four contained local news and advertising which were typeset in Everett and printed in Lock's shop. Pages two and three were boilerplates, "canned" newspaper features and national advertising, which Lock bought on a regular basis and which came already printed and folded on paper that fit his press.

In 1949 Lock got a job as principal at Quilcene on the Olympic Peninsula. His wife, Helen, also a teacher, stayed in Darrington to keep her teaching position. Thursday night Helen would gather the local news and advertising and take it to Everett to be typeset. On his way home from Quilcene on Friday for the weekend with his family, Frank would pick up the type. By breakfast time Saturday, after an all-night session in his print shop, Frank would have *The Darrington News* ready for mailing.

After a while the newspaper — which had never made a penny anyway — became too much for the family to keep up with. Lock and his wife just quit the publishing business with a big election issue as their final contribution to Darrington's journalistic history. [24]

It wasn't until April 1955 that Darrington once again had a newspaper. Cliff Danielson, then managing editor of the *Anacortes American*, decided to try a publishing venture for Darrington at the request of some business people there. Danielson continued to live and work in Anacortes, spending Saturday in Darrington. His one staff member was the late Thelma Crawford. Four or five country correspondents supplemented Thelma's and Danielson's work. The *Timber Bowl Tribune* was typeset and printed at the *Anacortes American* plant and mailed from there. There were 300 or 400 subscribers. In January or February 1956, Danielson had a chance to buy a paper in Eastern Washington. He turned the *Timber Bowl Tribune* over to Charles Dwelley, publisher of the *Concrete Herald*. No money changed hands in the turnover.[25]

In March 1956 Allison R. "Ace" Comstock, one of Dwelley's employees, moved to Darrington to take over the paper. Comstock was told he could have it for free. For four months Comstock and Dwelley handled the paper, printing it at the *Concrete Herald's* plant. Then the paper became a family affair with Ace's wife, Bernice, becoming half of the two-person writing-editing-publishing team.

The Comstocks purchased an old Cottrell hand-fed press. They set type on an ancient linotype machine and printed the paper in their own shop. The first shop was located near the old Pine Tree and later was moved to the old Pioneer Hotel. The press was delivered in pieces from Alexander Printing in Everett.

Ace and football coach George Jones reassembled it by intuition since neither of them had ever seen a press in pieces before.

Bernice recalled the first issue of the paper printed on the new press. The newly assembled press was not adjusted quite right. In front of many of Darrington's dignitaries, Bernice, then many months pregnant, had to catch the papers as they came flying off the press. She was soon surrounded by waist high stacks of crumbled papers as she tried to retrieve enough unspoiled copies for the 1,200 subscribers.

Bernice also recalled hand feeding Ace his dinner as he hand fed the press, not daring to stop the old piece of equipment long enough to eat his dinner. There was always the chance it wouldn't start up again.

The Comstocks continued the hectic job of publishing the *Tribune* for about two years. Then they sold their equipment to pay off some debts and left town. Their's was the last of Darrington's publishing ventures[26] until November 2, 1978, when Darrington postal patrons discovered *The Darrington Illustrated Press* in their boxes. Dick Brocious, who arrived in Darrington in late summer of 1978, is the one-man reporter, editor, photographer and publisher of the latest newspaper endeavor in town. The weekly paper is printed at the Sedro-Woolley *Courier-Times* plant.

Bob Galbraith operated this car as a stage or jitney between Arlington and Darrington starting in about 1916 or '17. As roads became more passable several other motor stage lines were set up between the two communities. Bob Galbraith is at the wheel. Morris Galbraith is on the running board. The car is a 1912 McLaughlin Buick built in Canada. Courtesy of Ward Woodward.

Chapter 9

The Tarheels

Newcomers to Darrington usually can't believe their ears as they stop to eat, to fill up a gas tank or to shop at a grocery store. The accent of the South is here, tucked away in this unlikely spot in the mountains in the far Northwest. It just happens that Darrington is part of two major settlement areas in the state of Washington where emigrants from southern Appalachia have been living ever since the turn of the century.[1]

A majority of the southerners in Darrington are "Tarheels,"[2] natives of North Carolina, but some hail from Georgia and Tennessee. The original emigrants came west during the early years of the century to Lyman and Hamilton and other communities on the Skagit, some of which are no longer in existence. As logging opened up in the Darrington area, they moved into the Sauk Valley and into Darrington itself. Many of these early families were related to one another or knew one another back in Jackson, Haywood, Swain and Macon counties, North Carolina. Some of the early emigrants and their children and grandchildren still go back and forth to "Tarheel," as they call it, to visit or to live for a time, and it is still common for families to encourage other clan members from back east to come west to find better jobs. As industry in the South has developed in recent years, however, this westward migration has slowed.

It was the lure of better pay that brought the first emigrants westward from the economically poor hills and hollows of Appalachia. Railroads provided an easy mode of transportation to the new country. Avery and Octavia Bryson[3] were in a group of twelve people who came by train from Cullowhee, North Carolina, in 1912, shepherded by Louis or Luke Parker who had made a quick trip to Hamilton to check out employment possibilities. Convinced that employment was good, Parker returned to Cullowhee to recruit others to join him in a western adventure. The trip took five days and cost forty dollars a person. They came, Octavia said, because in North Carolina "a man could make a dollar a day falling timber. Out here he could make not less than five dollars a day." They also came because the hardwood logging industry in Appalachia was declining; in the Northwest the softwood industry was really just entering its heyday.

For six years the Brysons lived in the Dempsey Lumber Co. camp near Hamilton where Avery had a job. Then in October 1919 the family moved to a farm on the Sauk Prairie. There the Brysons could do some marginal farming to supplement Avery's seasonal work in the woods. Many of the North Carolinians combined farming on a small scale with work in the woods, following a pattern they were accustomed to back east.

Of the twelve people who came west in 1912, Octavia believed that she and her husband were the only ones who remained permanently. When she died in 1972, Octavia had never even been back to North Carolina to visit. Though none of her family ever followed her west to settle, two of her husband's brothers also came west and settled in the Darrington area. There are many Brysons in the Darrington area today, some descendants of their clan and some from another Bryson family group.

Alta Reece Long[4] is another oldtimer born in North Carolina. Her family left Canton, North Carolina, in 1907 and moved to Lyman on the Skagit. Asked why her family came, Alta said her father, Mark Reece, liked to hunt, and this was the country in which to hunt. Both in Carolina and out toward the Prairie near Darrington Mark Reece kept bears, fattening them like hogs for the slaughter, until he was informed that it was against the law; then he quit bear-farming.

Alta was the first of her family to move from Lyman to the Darrington area. She came in 1916 with her husband, Tom, an emigrant from Georgia whose family originated in North Carolina. Tom and Alta settled on land that belonged to her father. Tom cut cedar off the land for shingle bolts, and they began stump farming. Alta and her son and daughter-in-law still farm the land, growing two or three immense gardens and tending a few chickens, ducks, cows and horses.

Alta and her husband went back to Georgia to visit but never to live. They didn't like it. For one thing it was too hot.

Pearl Lewis[5] was Tom Long's sister. She was born in Macon, North Carolina. She and her husband, Theodore, originally from Pickens Co., South Carolina, came to the Darrington area from Georgia in 1927. Both her brother and sister, Maude Bates, were living in the Darrington area then. Discouraged by the wet weather and a bit homesick they went back to the south for "two or three crops," trying to make a living on a cotton farm. The short stay back east convinced them that dreary weather or not, Washington was the place to live. In the summer in the Northwest you could sleep when the night came. Back in the South you lay awake and sweated. "If you weren't wet with sweat, the bed bugs kept you awake," Pearl recalled. The family returned to the Darrington area in 1934 and stayed. Theodore worked in the woods on the road building crew for Sauk River Lumber Co. Pearl took care of the farm and a growing family of eight children.

For the people from the South, having money was a new experience, and they distrusted any bank which would "take it." Pearl said that for years she wore her family's savings strapped around her waist in a specially made money belt. When a friend finally convinced her and her husband that Pearl's safety was in jeopardy with the money strapped to her, they agreed to bank it. There was almost enough in the belt to pay off their land and their house.

Minnie and Olan Cabe[6] came directly to Darrington from Franklin, North Carolina, in 1926. They were struggling to make a living on a small farm near there. They had friends and relatives in Darrington — the Sam Bateses, the Frank Brysons, Sr., the "Doc" Greens. The transplanted Tarheels kept writing about how much money a person could make in Darrington working in the woods. Olan and Minnie decided to come west. "It was just like home here," Minnie recalled in the summer of 1974. "There were people here from all around back there." Olan went to work for Sauk River Lumber Co. as a faller and bucker and worked twenty-eight years for them until his retirement. Olan died in 1972.

When Minnie and Olan came to Darrington, two traditions of the South were still faithfully kept by the emigrants. One was the tradition of the singing convention in which at least twice a year a choir from the First Baptist Church in Darrington participated with groups from Lyman, Hamilton, Mount Vernon, Sedro-Woolley, Clear Lake and other communities where there were enclaves of Tarheels for an all-day sing and food fest. The books they used were printed in "shaped" notes. You read the music, not so much by its position on the clef as by the shape of the note. (In the late 1960's when my husband was pastor at First Baptist Church, the choir still used some books with shaped notes and some of the choir members despaired if we sang from any other book; they couldn't read the music.)

Minnie recalled that choirs prepared faithfully for singing conventions, often meeting twice a week. Once the church even hired a singing teacher from Franklin, North Carolina, to come for three or four weeks of workshops in the traditional music of the South. "But that time's over now," Minnie lamented. "People don't have that much energy anymore."

It is true that the day of the big singing convention is over, but a few faithful Tarheels still meet together at various churches in the Skagit valley whenever a fifth Sunday falls in a month to sing together and play their guitars, banjos and fiddles "for the Lord."

Another tradition that has never entirely died is quilting. Minnie recalled that women used to get together often to quilt. "We'd quilt for circle (women's church group) and we'd quilt for one another." Once a month the women would gather at a friend's home to quilt for some member of the group. The hostess would kill a chicken and fix chicken and dumplings and biscuits for her working guests. They'd quilt, eat and quilt some more. Patterns which Minnie recalled working were Flower Garden with 144 flowers to a quilt; Friendship Fan, an appliqued quilt; and Double Wedding Ring, a pattern which Minnie had worked back home in Carolina. Minnie recalled the names of the regular quilters, all transplanted Southerners: Mrs Tom Stoney, Laura Mallonee, Maude Bates, Harriett Ensley and Eva Cogdill.

Chicken and biscuits and Tarheel beans — a special green bean always fixed with the right amount of bacon fat or salt pork for flavoring — are also part of the lasting tradition of Tarheel in Darrington. I had never eaten a good biscuit in my life until I tasted Maude Bates' biscuits the first year we lived in

Darrington. We had chicken too, that night, but those biscuits were something special, and I ate more than my share. Corn bread fixed by an oldtime Tarheel is a different experience, too, light and moist and not quite so sweet as my Northern recipes turn out.

It's hard to estimate how many first generation Tarheels still live in Darrington and its environs, but in 1947 there were 500 out of a population of 850 according to an old unidentified clipping I ran across in a Darrington scrapbook. Darrington was then, and in many ways still is, a Tarheel town and proud of it.

Dr. B.T. Blake was pictured in 1907 or 1908. Blake was Darrington's only physician until 1929. Photo by and courtesy of W. Ward Woodward.

Chapter 10

Small-Town Medicine

Through most of its growing-up years, Darrington's ills and injuries were cared for by two pioneers in country medicine, the late physicians Bayard Taylor Blake and Norwood C. Riddle. Between the two of them they cared for Darrington's people for sixty years.

Dr. B.T. Blake[1] came to Darrington in 1906, fresh out of medical school at the University of Vermont. Why he chose the West and a little town in the wilds, no one remembers; but he loved it and lived out his life here, never returning to his native New York State, and traveling back to New England only once in fifty years.

Dr. Blake was a short man, who grew more portly as the years piled up on him. Friends remember that his head was barely visible above the steering wheel of the car he owned. Though he used a car later in his practice, he found horses the only way to get around in the early days. He owned four horses, but his favorite was "Billy" who could be depended upon to swim the doctor across the Sauk and to travel many miles to patients in isolated cabins around the countryside. A special bond developed between Billy and the doctor, and in later years, as Dr. Blake's mind began to wander, he often talked about the horse as if Billy were still with him and ready to take him on another journey of mercy.

One of Dr. Blake's admirers was Dr. N.C. Riddle, who came in 1929 to take over some of Dr. Blake's medical practice. Dr. Riddle's assessment of Blake: "He was all you could ask for in a country doctor. He was an expert in 'rough and tumble' medicine."

"I learned so much from him," Dr. Riddle recalled in later years. "He was ingenious. He had lots of common sense. He knew a lot of things you'd never know from books. He could always devise a way to do a thing. It didn't make any difference when it was or where it was or whether he'd get anything out of it, he'd go when he was needed. He'd wade a creek or ride a horse or take an old ferry. But he'd go. And then when he got there he'd do something and the 'something' that was indicated."

When Blake came to Darrington he lived in a small house on the site of the present Darrington Hardware Store. It was to this home that he took his bride, Florence, who came from their hometown of Nicholvile, N.Y., to be married by the local Methodist pastor, A.B. Towne. Later Blake moved his office to the second floor of the Pioneer Hotel. Many people in Darrington recall being treated by the doctor there. Many were born in that small hospital in the hotel.

In 1916 or 1917 Dr. Blake acquired twenty acres of the U.S. Mill property. He converted the cookhouse into a hospital, another building on the property into a "pest house," or contagious disease ward, and another into a home for himself and his family.

At the time he acquired the hospital, Blake was a contract doctor for the logging camps and mills in the area. According to pharmacist Roy Wolfe, Blake had contracts to care for about 2,000 men. Under the contract system, a certain amount of money was taken out of a worker's pay each pay period for medical care. Ninety percent of the money went to the local doctor. Ten percent went to the State Department of Labor. This arrangement was only possible if a majority of the workers at a specific mill or camp agreed to the contract.

Though he was the workers' doctor and was the man who was called on to mend broken heads and bodies battered in logging, train and mill accidents, Blake's greatest joy was delivering babies. According to Pearl Wilson Hasenyager, who began as an emergency assistant to Dr. Blake in 1924 or '25, "Each baby was something wonderful new. Each one was kind of a thrill. He didn't lose many, but if he did, it sure hurt him deep."

Mrs. Hasenyager recalls that they had "some dandies" when it came to O.B. calls. "You didn't know where you were going or what you'd find when you got there," when the doctor called her and said, "Let's go."

"I still don't know where I went one time," she recalled with a chuckle. "It was 'way in the middle of the night. The house sat in an orchard. We only had lamplight to work with. Water was on the porch — cold water." There was a tent out in the yard, and it was into this tent that the grandmother herded the children — "I lost track of them" — when the doctor and Mrs. Hasenyager arrived. No one told them where anything was, but Blake and his assistant were good at improvising from anything that was at hand, and the baby was safely delivered.

Then there were the Whitall twins, known to Pearl and the doctor as "the flashlight twins." They were born while Mrs. Hasenyager held a flashlight so Dr. Blake could see what he was doing. Earlier that night a car had crashed into a light pole, knocking out all the lights in town. The family and the doctor only expected one baby, and Dr. Blake grew nervous when he realized that there were twins to be brought in to the darkened world. The second baby had to be turned, and Dr. Blake whistled tunelessly — he always did — as the nervous sweat poured off him. But all went well, and by morning light friends and relatives were awed and amazed at the *two* babies lying in the bassinet.

An expert at obstetrics, Dr. Blake also was known as a good surgeon. Mrs. Hasenyager and Dr. Riddle recalled assisting Blake in picking bone fragments from a couple of crushed heads — one from a block and tackle falling out of a tree, another from a train wreck — and successfully inserting silver plates. Blake used to say, "I'll tackle anything but a basic skull fracture, and I don't think there's anyone who can do anything for that."

Blake continued doing surgery even after losing one thumb in a wood-cutting accident. He could manage everything but the suturing, which Mrs. Hasenyager did for him. But his days of surgery came to an end when he cut off the second thumb as he cut wood another time. "If I had been drinking," he complained to his nurse, "I'd have thought I had that coming; but, Pearl, I was perfectly sober."

Dr. Blake had spunk that was appropriate to the pioneer life. One day when the river was high and the primitive cable-ferry across the Sauk wasn't running, Dr. Blake got an emergency call from across the river. Blake recruited an especially mean Indian to take him across in a canoe. Halfway across the Indian told Blake, "I'm going to drown you." Blake, who wasn't armed, reached inside his coat as if to get a gun. "Before you have a chance to do that I'll blow your brains out," he threatened. The Indian took no chances and proceeded to the other bank.

Blake's manner of speaking was expressive of the rural life he lived with his patients. "That boy squealed like a pig under a gate," he would say of a particularly noisy patient. "That fella's sick," he would say with a shake of his head. "He's puffed up like a poisoned pup."

The country doctor had a compassionate heart that made him extend himself beyond what many people might say are the bounds of caring. His successor, Dr. Riddle, claimed that he never had the spirit that Dr. Blake had. (Doc Riddle's patients will dispute that!)

Riddle told about the time that a woman and her three children arrived at the back door of the hospital one cold January afternoon. She told Dr. Riddle that she was leaving her husband and she wanted permission to live in Dr. Riddle's shed. No, said the young doctor, and he turned her away without suggesting any alternative plan. The woman then went to Dr. Blake's home nearby. Could she stay there in his shed? The doctor said yes. Later that night it got cold and snowed, and the woman began to get cold feet about leaving her husband. She asked Dr. Blake if he would take her and the children home. He did, driving ten or twelve miles to her home and back in a snow storm.

Pearl Hasenyager recalls with gratitude Blake's assuring presence the last three days of her chronically ill son's life. He stayed with her and the young man night and day, leaving only to take care of emergencies. "It wasn't what he did, it was just the feeling that he was here," she said. Dr. Blake, and later Dr. Riddle, stayed with her through major surgeries in hospitals in Everett. The two doctors were a lot alike, she said — doctor, friend, family counselor all combined.

Blake took seriously his medical oath to provide care for anyone who needed it. His daughters say that it may have been his insistence that even the town's reputed prostitutes deserved medical care that added to their mother's decision to leave Dr. Blake in 1922. Mrs. Hasenyager felt that life in the small, sometimes rough town was too hard on Florence. She was alone

Three prominent Darrington men were caught clowning in this picture taken about 1910. They are W. Ward Woodward, "Colonel" Jenkins, expressman on the Northern Pacific gas-powered car, and Dr. B.T. Blake. Courtesy of W. Ward Woodward.

much of the time, Mrs. Hasenyager said, and it must have been difficult on her.

Though he was a man devoted to other people's needs, Dr. Blake had burdens of his own. After Florence left him, taking their daughters Bessie and Mary with her, he moved into an apartment for a while. In about 1928 the discouraged man decided to leave Darrington, going to Mineral, Wash., for a year. But he could not bear to stay away from the town he had learned to love, and he returned.

Always a man who loved to drink, he became an alcoholic in later years. Toward the end of his life his mind failed him. Unable to care for himself, he was cared for for three years by Al Ritter, a gentle, cheerful male nurse. Ritter was cook, housekeeper, chauffeur, companion and nurse. Bessie and Mary recalled Ritter with great love. "He took such good care of Dad," they said. "He was a grand guy." For the last months of his life Dr. Blake was a patient at Northern State Hospital in Sedro-Woolley, Wash., where he died December 22, 1951, just two days before his seventy-third birthday.

One of the town's proudest memories of Dr. Blake is of sending him to the World Series in Boston in 1946. Blake was an ardent baseball fan. He had a specially-designed board he used to record plays as he listened to baseball games on the radio.

Through personal gifts and benefit ball games the townspeople raised over $1,300 to send the old doctor to the World Series. The late Royal Brougham of the *Seattle Post-Intelligencer* was instrumental in getting tickets where there weren't any available! Dr. Blake flew east, becoming somewhat of a nationwide celebrity as he was interviewed by newspapers at airports across the country and given a special national tribute on the radio show "Kate Smith Speaks."

In 1929 another colorful, dedicated doctor came to Darrington. He was Dr. Riddle [2], a man who had tried out medical practice in the big cities of the East and Midwest and found life there "full of hypocrites." Partly to find his own niche in life and partly to find a place more agreeable with his wife's health, Dr. Riddle moved west, responding to the old Everett Clinic's call for a man to take up Blake's abandoned contract work in Darrington.

Riddle held a common heritage with many of the people who lived in Darrington: He was from North Carolina. Born in 1890, he had been raised on a farm near Jonesboro, Moore County. He

Dr. Blake takes care of another kind of patient, a pet bear cub. The photo was taken about 1910. Photo by and courtesy of Ward Woodward.

left the farm to go to college because the farm "wasn't big enough."

He graduated from the University of North Carolina and received his medical degree from Jefferson Medical College, Philadelphia, Pa., in 1919. His internship was in New York City. For a short time he practiced medicine in Harnett County, N. C., with J. W. Haford. But country practice in his home state couldn't satisfy the young man. He signed on as a company doctor for a mining firm and sailed for Peru. He stayed four years.

When he came back to the States in 1926 he decided he'd like to study orthopedics. His dream was to become an orthopedic surgeon. However, as time went on, he was to find his dream frustrated by failing eyesight, even as a young man. For the next two or three years Dr. Riddle moved around restlessly from one orthopedic hospital to another. At Shriner's Hospital in Chicago he met Carol Busk, assistant superintendent of nurses, and the woman who would become his wife in 1929.

"I had an itch in the heel," Dr. Riddle said, as he recalled those early years. He kept moving. Erie and Pittsburgh, Pa. Then finally Niagara Falls, N. Y. In January 1929 Riddle married his nurse-sweetheart in Niagara Falls. But being married didn't cure his restlessness. Riddle didn't like Niagara Falls. He kept searching for someplace he could be happy. That was when he heard about Darrington. He and "Chink," or "Chinquapin" as he called hs wife, made the big and lasting decision to move west.

Carol was disappointed with Darrington, but she took solace from the fact that there was a depot and a railroad track. Riddle loved it and they stayed.

The doctor had hoped to start practice immediately, being given reciprocity for his New York medical license; but Washington State required that he take the medical exams. He had three or four days to prepare for the exams covering the first two years of medical school which he had completed fourteen years before. Those done, he was required to take the last two years' exams. He studied at night and took the exams during the day. Riddle wasn't sure that he passed all those exams covering microscopic hystology, pathology and anatomy. But he was confident about the exam in clinical practice. He got his license.

Dr. Boyd Collier was temporarily replacing Blake at the Darrington Hospital when Dr. Riddle arrived. Collier stayed on for ten or twelve days to help Dr. Riddle become familiar with the hospital and its operation. Collier also took Riddle to some of the logging camps in the area for which Riddle now held the medical contracts. It was on one of these trips that Riddle met one of the amusing characters he loved to tell about in later years.

When they got on the speeder to ride to the Sauk River Logging Camp one day, Riddle recalled that there was a "great big feller in a Stetson hat, with a red bandana around his neck, two .38's at his waist and cowboy boots on his feet."

"It's all right," Collier reassured Riddle. "That's Tex. He's harmless."

No one knew where Tex Leroy came from. No one knew how many of his stories were true. But co-workers said that on Sundays he would take a western novel and a saddle out into the woods. He'd throw the saddle over a fallen tree and sit there reading his book. Every once in a while he'd shoot off his guns. Then, putting them back in his holsters, he'd pick up the book and read some more.

Soon after Riddle took up practice in Darrington, Tex was brought to his door one midnight. "The old ticker stopped a while ago," he said dramatically. "I had to get up and jump up and down to get it started."

Riddle told him that his heart probably hadn't stopped. He probably just had eaten something that didn't agree with him, but to make sure, he kept Tex in the hospital for observation. Poor Tex. He was sure he was going to die and turned over all his worldly goods to the nurse.

Riddle recalled Dr. Blake's return to Darrington. Unannounced, the old doctor strolled in one day and introduced himself. Riddle had heard a lot about the "old doc," as he called him. They got to talking and found that they liked each other. Blake didn't begrudge Riddle his practice. "He was too big a man to hold a grudge," Riddle said. "I had come here and taken over his place, he didn't hold that against me . . . We had a darn good time. I just liked him for what he was and what he could do and his mannerisms and good will and knowledge. I got to thinking, 'If anyone gets driven out of here, it'll be me!' "

For a time Riddle rented the hospital from the Blakes and then bought it. It became known then as "Dr. Riddle's hospital" and remains known by that name, though it has been converted into apartments. Blake continued a small private practice in town. Riddle held the contracts and manned the hospital. The men often worked together on emergencies. "I don't like this thing of two doctors in the same town not on speaking terms," Dr. Riddle said.

Dr. Riddle had a witty sense of humor and a willingness to give his opinion no matter how caustic. "I think if you can't laugh at yourself, life's hardly worth living," he said once. "I don't like to see a person who's too serious." The stories he shared about his life in Darrington often indicated the humor he saw in the midst of pain.

John D. and a man named Sullivan were patients at the same time in the hospital. John D. was "big, uncouth, stupid and ignorant," in Riddle's opinion. He had a broken leg, injured in a logging accident. Sullivan was hospitalized with a fractured hip. The two loggers shared a room.

John had an old book which he read for hours every day. Now Sullivan knew that John really couldn't read, so whenever John left the room, Sullivan would move the bookmark back a hundred pages or so. John would come back, pick up the book and keep reading.

Every time John left the room his roommate did the same thing. And every time John came back, he'd pick up the book and start reading at the place Sullivan had marked. John never did catch on to what was happening, because he commented to the nurse one day, "This gol-darned book! I'll never get through it!"

Riddle got most of his patients from the woods or mills, but he also got quite a bit of business from the taverns. He told the story of one man who had been injured in the woods and had had a long stay at the hospital. When the man was about ready to be released, he begged Dr. Riddle to let him go up town one evening. Riddle reluctantly consented with the warning to come back early.

Well, the man did come back early, early in the morning, that is. And he was in almost worse shape than the accident in the woods had put him in. "He looked like he had been run through some kind of a machine," Riddle said. "I've never seen a fellow so beat up and dishevelled."

"Tavern patients" found that the doctor had little sympathy for them. Going on the assumption that they were sufficiently anesthesized, Dr. Riddle reportedly wasted little gentleness on them as he sewed or patched their brawl-caused wounds. But even men who received "the tavern treatment" held no grudges

A portly Dr. Blake in the 1930's stands on the porch of the Darrington Hospital which he sold to Dr. N. C. Riddle in 1929. Courtesy of Pearl Wilson Hasenyager.

against the doctor. "He was just trying to teach us a lesson," one tavern patient said.

Both Riddle and Blake had to fight medical superstition among the people they served. "There used to be a common belief among laymen that if a doctor could get you to sleep, he'd amputate for practice," Riddle said. One fellow came in with a big gash in his leg. Dr. Riddle suggested that they use anesthesia before working on the leg. "Oh, no you don't," the injured man protested. "You get me to sleep, you'll take my leg off." So Drs. Riddle and Blake proceeded without anesthesia.

Riddle was a listener. He believed that a patient needed to be listened to. That was part of the treatment. He said one of his professors had told him, "If a patient wants to diagnose himself for half an hour, let him. You listen. Then when he's through, do what *you* think best. That's good medical practice."

Riddle's ability to listen and his well-developed sense of touch extended his service as a physician and confidante even into the total blindness that plagued him as an older man. He would sit at the old roll-top desk which had also been Dr. Blake's and listen as his friends and old patients told him their troubles or shared some humor of the day.

Dr. Riddle's training in orthopedics was put to good use in Darrington, where broken bones could be expected in logging accidents. He was an expert cast maker. Pearl Hasenyager recalls with amusement the pail in which Dr. Riddle mixed plaster for his casts. She used to tease him that he kept putting plaster on until he could see the bottom of the pail.

"When he set up an ankle or wrist, it would look like it was in an awkward position," she said. "But when you got through with it, you could use it. Another thing I used to say was 'That cast's not coming off of there 'til you *cut* it off."

Mrs. Hasenyager told about a boy who broke his elbow in a fall while on a summer vacation near Darrington. Dr. Riddle set the elbow and built one of his casts around it. The boy's family was from Seattle, so Dr. Riddle suggested they check his work out with an orthopedic physician there. The family did. The specialist took one look at the cast and exclaimed, "That man knows his casts!"

→

Dr. Norwood C. Riddle, Darrington's physician from 1929 until 1966, was photographed at his roll top desk at the Darrington Hospital sometime in the 1950's. Courtesy of Pearl Wilson Hasenyager.

Riddle also had some favorite liniments and cough syrups which he had developed and which the local pharmacist mixed and kept on hand for him. Riddle also had a very well-stocked pharmacy room in the hospital from which he dispensed many medicines.

Riddle was never a know-it-all kind of physician. Many Darrington people remember him with gratitude for the things he would *not* do. He would send his patients to specialists if he felt their condition called for it, and he was unafraid to seek another physician's aid. "I don't like a doctor who knows it all," he said. "In this business of medicine, one man *can't* know it all."

From 1928 to 1944 Ellen Olson Pollard was nurse at the Darrington Hospital. She worked briefly with Dr. Blake, was there during Dr. Collier's short stay, and continued as Dr. Riddle's nurse until 1944. Miss Olson, who married Ed Pollard in 1942, lived at the hospital in a small apartment and answered calls night and day. She received her room and board and $75 a month. She got every other weekend off.

Evenings at the hospital could be long and tedious when things were quiet. Often Dr. Riddle, his nurse, a neighbor and one of the patients would play cards. Mrs. Pollard recalled with amusement that the only time she ever saw Dr. Riddle really get upset was when he felt someone had tricked him out of winning.

One of Mrs. Pollard's other memories is that she was the only person ever to be isolated in the pest house for scarlet fever.

Dr. Riddle's one major recreation was his garden. The large garden plot was a source of supply for the hospital pantry for many years. Then after the hospital was discontinued, Dr. Riddle kept the garden for his and his family's own enjoyment and to keep his friends supplied. Between office calls he would slip into overalls and boots and work for a few minutes, only to be called back in by Mrs. Hasenyager to see another patient.

As he got older, his wife wondered if the garden work wasn't too much for him. "No," said his nurse, "That's the only recreation he has; don't take that away from him."

One fall, after he was blind, he asked Mrs. Hasenyager to go buy him some overalls and find his short-handled cultivating tool. It was time to dig potatoes, and he wanted to do the job. Mrs. Hasenyager found some striped overalls at the hardware store, and brought them back for the doctor to put on. She took him to the garden and left him alone to dig potatoes on his hands and knees, close to the earth he loved.

Dr. Riddle faced the debilities of old age and the restrictions of blindness with the same mixture of humor, philosophy and just plain grit that had been his trademark throughout life. He wrote at the time he turned seventy-five:

> Unlike Winston Churchill at seventy-five, I do not feel that I am ready to meet my Maker, and I am sure that He feels that there is always unfinished work that you may putter around and help do. There may be a bit of a lift one may offer some young, worthy person . . . Age as we look at it at my age is considered and has always been a great liability. But is it? There never has been or can be a complete liability any more than there can be a complete asset.

> Why should one decry the fact that he has been reasonably healthy and active enough to grow old? Isn't it a time for tolerance, great patience and consideration for others? One knows that the moon is unattainable for him even though the present generation seems to have different ideas. Who wants or needs sympathy or pity at seventy-five or at twenty-five? For if that is all one is looking for, he is finished at any age.

He told a news reporter at the time of his retirement in 1966 that he would have liked to wait a little longer to retire, but he couldn't see that it would get him anything. He said his attitude was like that of Art Anderson, the old Darrington storekeeper, who used to say, when people asked him why he was so happy, "Happy? I'm just whistling to keep from crying!"

After total blindness had come, Dr. Riddle typed out his thoughts on "What to Remember When We Have Lost One of Our Main Senses." In comments that read like an introspective pep talk, Riddle wrote:

> I find that one has to fight against the tendency to brood or mope and the tendency to pity yourself for your plight as this will serve to spoil the parade. Be thankful that you have your mind and other faculties to bank upon and that you have had a comparatively long and useful life up to this time and that there are many more unfortunate creatures who are not crying . . . Nobody likes a long face or long story of grievances or self pity. Let the mouth corners turn up and not down!

136

The determination to live and be useful continued for Dr. Riddle through the death of his daughter, Barbara, the rearing of two grandchildren in his old age, the frustration of blindness, the illnesses of his wife, and, at the very end of his own life, a broken hip. One visitor to the convalescent center where Dr. Riddle was recuperating from the hip fracture found him determinedly raising and lowering his legs as he sat in a chair in a painful effort to regain full use of his legs.

Dr. Riddle died on Feb. 1, 1973, with his faithful assistant, Pearl Hasenyager beside him. He is buried in the Arlington Cemetery. His epitaph most properly is the sign he had posted on his office door at the Darrington Hospital:

1929-1939
Country Doctor
Office hours — anytime

1939-1949
General Practitioner
Hours 8-12   2-8

1949-1959
Internist
Hours 1-12   2-4
No Night Calls

1959-1969
Blind Consultant
Office Hours:
Catchin' Before Hangin'

Chapter 11

Big Timber

As the country around Darrington opened up in the late 1800's not only did adventurers, prospectors and settlers see rich opportunities there; so did the U.S. government. In 1897 President Grover Cleveland added to the already established Pacific Forest Reserve, setting aside forest acreage in what was called the Washington Forest Reserve. This proclamation put the mountains and natural resources around Darrington in the custody of the U.S. government and placed some limits on activities within the boundaries.

The action disturbed oldtimers who were used to doing as they pleased on the land. One old prospector and miner, D.D. Beese, who had lived on the North Fork of the Stillaguamish for 21 years, reacted publicly to the proclamation:

I believe that the (forest) reserve was created for the benefit of a few lily-fingered gentlemen who want a place to hunt and fish. I can imagine no other reason. For twenty-one years I have been prospecting and mining and in all the camps combined which I have visited there was not so much mineral in sight as in Silverton. The White Horse district on the North Fork of the Stillaguamish River and the Buckeye Gulch are as rich as Silverton. All these are included in the reserve. If Cleveland comes to fish in that district, the miners will give a party and the guest of honor will wish he stayed away. [1]

138

Cleveland didn't come, but in 1898, Arthur Moll, a young homesteader on the Sauk River near Bedal, was appointed Darrington district forest ranger. Headquarters were at his homestead about eighteen miles upriver from Darrington. Moll's job was to patrol the trails and wagon roads in the forest, put out fires and do some basic trail construction and maintenance.

Moll's daughter, Frances Moll Murray Soper[2], recalled the story of the family's move to the homestead. Her parents were on horses. A third horse carried kitchen supplies on one side in a pack box and two-year-old Frances on the other. As they crossed the Sauk, the horse on which she was being packed failed to follow the lead horses and started downstream. "Mother had a fit; Father was beside himself," she said, but Moll managed to retrieve the horse with its precious cargo.

Life at the ranger's headquarters was lonely for Moll's young, well-educated wife. She longed to be able to talk with other women and often would go to her gate to try to converse with the Indian women as they passed by. "Mother said that the Indian women would talk, talk, talk and laugh among themselves as they pointed at us. (A baby brother had joined the family.) Their's were such nice fat babies, and we were so small. Mother said she almost felt ashamed."

For little Frances life at the homestead was exciting. She found the miners an interesting group of men. She recalled that one man always carried his gold in his pockets. Her father was afraid someone would hold him up. Another man returned from a supply trip to Darrington with a sack of sugar. When he got to his cabin he discovered a skunk had made himself at home while he was gone. He caught the skunk in an empty sugar sack. Then in his excitement he somehow grabbed the wrong bag and drowned the sugar, not the skunk, in the river!

Moll served as ranger until 1905. Then, bowing to his wife's requests to move to a civilized place, he went to Everett to work in the mills before settling his family in Arlington where he and his wife's cousin ran a hardware-furniture store for many years.

Charles Armstrong and John Atkins succeeded Moll for short periods of time until George Bradner was appointed ranger in 1908.[3] Under Bradner's administration, the first permanent

The first Darrington District Ranger Station was built at Clear Creek near Darrington. Photo was taken sometime between 1910 and 1914 when the station was moved to town. Courtesy of W. Ward Woodward.

Clear Creek Ranger Station
Snoqualmie National Forest
J. R. Brackett Dist Ranger

Darrington district ranger headquarters were constructed at Clear Creek. Headquarters remained at Clear Creek until 1914 when the Randall House in Darrington (at the corner of North Emens Avenue and Price Street) was rented for use as the district office. Later land was purchased in that part of town and a large Forest Service compound was developed.

During the early years of the Snoqualmie National Forest, as it was then called, when distances were longer because of lack of roads and trails, substations were built at French Creek, Sauk, Verlot, Hemple, Silverton and Barlow Pass. In those early days, the Darrington district's southern boundaries encompassed what was to become the Monte Cristo district in 1936. As time went on, boundaries moved and changed and Darrington district took in what had been the Suiattle-Finney Creek district with ranger stations at Blue Bird and Texas Pond and district headquarters at the site of old Sauk City at the confluence of the Sauk and Skagit Rivers.

Work of the early rangers in the Washington Forest Reserve and later in the National Forest was primarily in the areas of fire duty, trail construction and maintenance and some campground development. To facilitate fire watch, lookouts were established throughout the district, the first one being built on Gold Hill in 1915. That lookout, manned by Rowland Atcheson, was abandoned the same year. The following year a primitive lookout was established on Jumbo with Atcheson once again in charge.

Other lookouts were established on Mt. Pugh, 1921; Mt. Higgins, 1926; Three Fingers, 1930; French Point, 1934; White Chuck Bench, 1935; North Fork Bench, 1936; Red Mountain, 1936; Glacier Ridge, 1936; and Johnson Mountain, 1938. Miles and miles of telephone line were strung between the early lookouts and the district headquarters to facilitate reporting fires.

Nels Bruseth was the fire guard on Mt. Pugh the first season. The lookout was on the almost inaccessible top of the mountain. A strenuous hike up the mountain was capped by a climb of several hundred feet up a rope ladder. When Bruseth was lookout there, he was courting Beate Staff Falk, a young Norwegian girl who was lodging with her aunt and uncle Nicolai Aall at Bedal. Nels would finish his work in early evening, climb down the mountain, hike to Bedal, visit Beate and hike back to his post. "Most men have difficulty making that trip one way in a

day," former district ranger Harold Engles recalled as he told of
Nels' successful courtship.

In 1906 and 1907 during Theodore Roosevelt's administration, national forests were cautiously opened up for more
varied usage. In 1907 Roosevelt allowed that ripe timber in
limited amounts would be made available for sale. In the
Darrington District, the first U. S. Forest contract was made with
the Hazel Mill Co. in August 1908 for 7,860,000 board feet of fir,
hemlock, and cedar located on 320 acres on French Creek.[4]

Though the forest service had tied up much of the timber in
the area, there were still considerable stands of privately owned
timber that would be logged into the early 1950's.

Sound Timber Co. moved into the Stillaguamish valley below
Darrington near Whitehorse in 1916.[5] That first year the
company employed about 125 men as it began to cut 125 million
board feet of cedar and fir on 2,480 acres of privately owned land
on Squire Creek. The railroad spur which carried logs out from
the logging works connected with the Northern Pacific Branch at
the Fortson School.

As Sound logged below the town, it also began building a
railroad spur from Darrington north and across the Sauk River
to begin logging the virgin growth surrounding the Sauk Prairie.

With Sound Timber Co. in full operation in the fall of 1916,
log traffic on the Darrington Branch of the Northern Pacific
reached the highest peak in its history to that point. *The
Arlington Times* reported on October 19, 1916 that the
Darrington train had come in in two sections of forty cars each.
Both sections were made up almost entirely of logs. A night
logging train was to be added if railroad cars were available,
since the Rucker Brothers on Boulder Creek would begin
shipping in two weeks, augmenting the already historical load the
line was carrying. This was the era of shortages of railroad cars,
and at times the railroads' failure to supply adequate numbers of
cars closed down logging operations for weeks at a time.

Sound Timber continued to operate in the Darrington area
until 1944 when it sold out to Washington Veneer which later was
bought by Georgia-Pacific. Georgia-Pacific finished logging
private holdings about ten years later and left the valley.

Another company which moved into the Darrington area
about the same time as Sound Timber was Danneher. The first
Danneher camp was located a short distance north of the present
town limits. The Danneher Co. was later bought out by another

outfit headed by Fred MacFarland and renamed Andron for the rail stop near which the camp was located. Andron left the valley before 1930, finishing up on holdings above the Sauk Prairie. It was the first of the early large logging outfits to leave.

Sound and Danneher moved into the Darrington area at a time of unrest among the loggers and woodworkers of the Pacific Northwest. Industrial Workers of the World (IWW), or Wobblies, as they were called, were striking camps throughout the Puget Sound area in an effort to gain some specific rights and benefits. The Sound and Danneher camps took two different routes as a result of the Wobbly agitation. Danneher bowed to Wobbly demands and became the only thoroughly Wobbly camp and the longest Wobbly holdout in the Puget Sound area. After a blanket-burning incident at the camp, Mr. Danneher announced that the camp would supply full bedding and would only charge for laundering sheets and pillowcases, a major change in logging camp practice of that day. This was only one of the concessions Danneher made to what were considered radical demands.

Tom Tathum,[6] who worked for Danneher from 1919 to 1926, said that the camp was the first to have an eight-hour day with time and half for overtime. Danneher also made a practice of dividing a sick man's wages among the remaining crew members who were required to pick up the man's work.

Mr. Danneher himself was found dead under mysterious circumstances at the pier near his mill in Tacoma a few years after the Wobbly strikes. According to Tom Tathum's recollection, Danneher reportedly was found drowned, tied to a piling by a rope around his neck with his hands bound behind his back. The death was called a suicide, but Tathum and Toby Freese, who worked briefly for Danneher before the strike in 1917, felt the man was murdered, possibly by other camp or mill owners who disagreed with his liberal labor practices.

In contrast, the Sound Camp, with a shortage of workers following the Wobbly strike, became the first camp in the county to employ soldier loggers from the misnamed "Spruce Production Division" of the U.S. Signal Corps. Sixty soldier loggers were employed in the summer of 1918.

That summer, a Capt. Bickford in charge of the Loyal Legion of Loggers and Lumbermen visited the Danneher Camp and announced that open shop conditions would prevail there from that time on. A number of Loyal Legion Loggers were employed, and to doubly insure that the Wobbly regime would be ended,

143

seventy-two soldiers from the Spruce Production Division were placed at the camp in July. The soldiers remained at the Danneher and Sound Camps until just before Christmas 1918.

Other smaller logging camps operating in the Darrington area during the period of 1916 to 1925 were the Washington Spar and Lumber Co. (located on the way to Clear Creek at what is called Punkintown); McNeeley and Anderson (near Whitehorse, 1916); McCaughey and Leatherdale (logging 200 acres on Squire Creek with mill nearby, 1923); Klement and Kennedy (logging on Whitehorse west of Moose Creek with a mill at Fortson, 1925).

In 1920, the U. S. Forest Service announced plans for logging government land in a 130,000-acre working circle in the Upper Stillaguamish and Sauk River Valleys. A yearly cut of 40-50 million board feet was expected initially with the possibility of expanding to as much as 80 million board feet a year. Reforestation plans were included in the announced timber harvesting program.

Two years later the Forest Service announced a large sale of government timber on 5,800 acres on the Sauk. The acreage included 200 million board feet of douglas fir, silver fir, cedar and hemlock. The government land adjoined private holdings which would place the yield in the unit at 400 million board feet. The group reportedly interested in the sale was headed by N. C. Jamison of Everett and W. C. Butler, an Everett banker. Two months later the Everett-based group with Jamison and A. H. B. Jordan as chief stockholders, acquired the desired twenty-year contract, and the Sauk River Lumber Co. began its long life in the Darrington area.

While a railroad was being built up the Sauk to invade the first unit to be cut, the Sauk River Lumber Co. began building the largest and most modern movable logging camp the Puget Sound area had ever seen. The entire camp was constructed on flat cars so that it could be moved from location to location as logging progressed. The camp included twenty-six bunkhouses, each large enough to accommodate eight men and equipped with bunks, lavatory, stove and hot and cold running water. There were dining rooms and kitchens, an office, light plant, filing room and blacksmith shop and other necessary shops and storerooms all on wheels.

The company also announced plans to develop a permanent community on forty acres on the south edge of town where it envisioned forty-eight homes, an office and a 3,000-square-foot warehouse, all served by water and sewer systems. None of the houses that were planned were built, nor were the water and sewer systems ever developed, but the warehouse and office were completed within a year.

In February 1923, the company began logging with a crew of about 150 men. Within a short time the crew had grown to between 250 and 275 men. The portable camp, constructed near Darrington close to where the Washington Spar was located was moved five times during the next thirty years before it was finally hauled back to Darrington and dismantled. The camp was first moved to a place near the old covered bridge at the mouth of the White Chuck River in 1923; to Mary Smith's on the Sauk in 1925 or '26; to Dan's Creek in 1929; to Bedal in 1936; back to White Chuck in 1943; and back to Darrington in 1952 or '53. Back at the starting point, many of the buildings were bought by local people and moved to permanent sites where, singly or connected together, they are still used for lodging.

Chris Gilson was the first superintendent of operations for the Sauk Co. He had formerly headed the Florence Logging Co. work down the Stillaguamish Valley. Gilson was succeeded in 1923 by Dave Mallonee.[7] Mallonee was originally from Webster or Sylva, North Carolina, having come west shortly after the turn of the century. He worked for many years doing general logging and then worked as foreman for the Skagit Mill Co. with headquarters at Lyman on the Skagit River before moving to the Port Angeles area to head operations for the Puget Sound Timber Co.

Many people believe Mallonee was the man who "brought" North Carolinians to Darrington. Indirectly that might be true, but the story of Mallonee's part in the Tarheel migration to Darrington goes like this:

When Mallonee worked for Skagit Mill, he mentioned to Superintendent Sherman "Shorty" Davis that times were hard back in North Carolina and that men were needing work. Davis

--->

Yarder, left, and duplex (loader), right, of the Sauk River Lumber Co. were working near where the trail takes off to Mt. Pugh on the North Fork of the Sauk River in 1927 or '28. In lower row only identified man is Red Thurlow, second from left, the scaler. In the long row, man second from left is Johnny Mathis, next three are unidentified, then Lester Parker (yarding machine operator), Merlin "Tug" Thomas, Orry Snyder and Joe Stoney. The three men in the short row are unidentified. Photo by Darius Kinsey. Photo and identifications courtesy of Joe Stoney.

was so impressed with Mallonee's ability as a logger that he wanted more workers like him. Davis convinced John Hightower, company owner, to provide transportation from North Carolina and housing for families when they arrived. According to "Shorty's" son, Don Davis, three train car loads of Tarheels were brought out. Most of the men worked for the Skagit Mill, but others drifted to other camps on the Skagit and over to the Darrington area as logging opened up there.

Mallonee, in the meantime, had gone to work at Port Angeles. It was from there that he came in 1923, bringing with him only one other Tarheel, Burke Henson,[8] a man from Cullowhee, N. C., whom Mallonee had hired at Port Angeles a few years earlier. Shortly after starting work at Sauk, Mallonee directed Henson to write to Burl Ensley, another Carolinian, to ask him to come and be camp foreman. As far as Henson knows, he and Burl Ensley are the only Tarheels Mallonee was directly responsible for bringing to the Darrington area.

Henson was a "bull bucker," the man in charge of a crew of sixty to eighty-five fallers, buckers and scalers.[9] All of the falling and bucking was done with hand saws when Henson started out. When he finished work in the 1950's power saws were in use.

Fallers and buckers were paid so much a thousand board feet, or by the bushel, as it was called. The going rate was forty, forty-five, or fifty cents per thousand, which meant that a man could make $8 to $12 a day. "That was good pay at the time," Henson said. "But it was killing work, awfully hard work." The method of pay often led to competition among the crew, and as saws flew and the timber fell, accidents caused by speed and carelessness were frequent.

A faller was a skilled workman. "You had to know how to fall a tree to save it," Henson recalled. During his working days, the longest tree saved without a break in it was 248 feet tall. In those days men with crosscut saws were falling fir that was from four to nine feet in diameter and cedar that was sixteen or seventeen feet across. It was the era of the big timber.

This huge pile of logs was the work of a col' deck donkey. The machine piled the logs as they were cut. Then the logs were rigged to a skyline and hauled to a major yarding-loading site downhill. There were often two col' deck donkeys operating on a side (logging unit). This photo was taken in May 1937 on the North Fork of the Sauk near the present Bedal campground. Photo by Darius Kinsey. Courtesy of Joe Stoney.

148

Tom Ashe,[10] Burke Henson's brother-in-law, came to Darrington from Sylva, North Carolina in 1928. He went to work as a hook tender and side foreman for about eight dollars a day. (The hook tender was the head man in the brush, directing yarding operations from there. Yarding is the term used to describe moving logs via cables to a landing where they can be loaded onto railroad cars, or today, onto trucks. A side is one logging unit. Sauk operated as many as four logging units at one time.)

Ashe and Henson combined to describe the workers and equipment assigned to a side:

Hook tender — head man in the brush; directed yarding operations from the brush.

Riggin' slinger — showed which logs to get; gave signal to go ahead or stop yarding operation.

Four chokermen — set chokers (cables) around logs to yard them in to the landing.

Powder monkey — blew holes under logs so chokermen could put cables around them.

High rigger — rigged spar trees and laid out cables, block and tackle.

Second rigger — high rigger's helper.

Two engineers — ran donkey (yarder) and duplex (loader).

Chaser — unhooked logs at landing after they were yarded in.

Head loader — showed second loaders (assistants) which logs to put tongs on in order to load them onto railroad cars.

Three second loaders — assisted head loader.

Night watchman — slept on the machines. Got up early to fire up the steam equipment to have it ready for crew, then went back to camp when crew arrived.

Firemen — kept the boilers fired up during the day.

Whistle punk — signaled for yarding operations with steam whistle.

----------→

A skidder, combining a loader (on left) and yarder (on right) in one unit, was used by Sauk River Lumber Co. This unit was located at what was called the Cougar Creek setting, past Lost Creek on the North Fork of the Sauk. It was junked after being used at this setting in May 1940. Upper row, left to right: Unidentified, Leighton Cabe, Virgil Inman, Tommy Tathum. Lower row, left to right, Grady Morris, Jim Black, crew boss or rigger unidentified, unidentified, Howard Inman, Hank Rogers, D. Jones, unidentified, unidentified, Horace McCracken, Bill Barker, Donald Jones, Joe Stoney, Elmer Cabe, Bob Stoney. Photo by Darius Kinsey. Photo and identifications courtesy of Joe Stoney.

In those days 8,000 to 10,000 board feet (b.f.) of logs were put on a railroad car, the average being around 8,000 board feet. One train could handle sixty to seventy cars. As Tom Ashe said, "We took out more in a day than these guys today take out in a week." Henson said that from 1925 to 1929 Sauk took out from one to 1.2 million board feet of timber every two days.

Besides the crew of fallers, buckers and scalers and the crew operating a side, there were other workers who were essential to the railroad logging operation. There was the road construction crew which prepared the right of way and grade for the railroad. There was the steel gang which laid the railroad and took it up as needed. The main line was laid permanently. Spurs into logging units were lifted when logging was completed in one area and were moved to the next area. Gandy-dancers worked on the main line of the railroad as engineers, firemen.

Most important to the morale of the camp was the cookhouse crew. Many a logger has quit a camp because of the food, but at the Sauk Camp that apparently was not a problem. Lawrence "Brick" West,[11] who worked for Sauk from 1926-1939, especially remembers cook Tom Tomlin. "He could make anything taste good," West recalled. Drummers (traveling salesmen) made it a point to be in camp at meal time to enjoy Tomlin's hearty cooking. When Brick West left Sauk to move to Sound Timber Co. as camp foreman in 1939, he "stole" Tom Tomlin. West, a heavy man even in retirement, patted his ample frontage and put the blame on Tom Tomlin.

West was one of the "home guards," one of the sixty or seventy Sauk River Lumber Co. men who lived in town with their families and who rode the speeder each morning up to camp and back at night. The men rode in a covered car which was pulled by a speeder. The speeder left town at six each morning and returned between six and midnight each night. Many men who were looking for work rode the speeder up to camp. Some rode for as long as two weeks before either giving up or getting hired.

West was head loader most of the time he worked for Sauk. He is a logger at heart, and his life has been one long working

This is what the movable logging camp used by the Sauk River Lumber Co. looked like. Almost all the buildings were built on railroad car beds and were moved from site to site as necessary. The camp was moved six times during the 30 years Sauk operated in the Darrington area. Photo by Darius Kinsey. Courtesy of Tom Ashe.

relationship with timber. He was nine or ten years old when he took his first job as a skid greaser at a shingle bolt camp at White Chuck on the Sauk. He got one dollar a day and board and room for keeping the wooden skids slippery enough for horses to drag cords of shingle bolts from the woods to the river edge where they were dumped into the water to be floated to mills downstream.

At thirteen he was working nights in the Lyman Timber Co. mill at Hamilton on the Skagit while he went to school during the day. When he finished eighth grade he went to work full time at the mill, but he never liked it. At eighteen he married and took his bride to Darrington where he began working for Sauk. He was back in the woods and loved it. "Once you're a logger, you're a logger all your life," he said. "It gets into your system. There's something different happening every day. Every place you go, there's something different about it. Mill work is boring. Every piece of timber that comes by is the same."

West stuck with the woods, moving to Sound Timber in 1939 to serve as camp foreman until 1951. Then he began a new era, that of a "gyppo," or independent logger, working with his sons. At first they salvaged logs along right of ways. Later they bid on small Forest Service contracts and contracted to work for some of the larger truck logging outfits. West retired in 1971 but even then continued to help his son from time to time in the small logging operation they had started together.

The good or bad fortune of a logger depends on nature's whims as well as on man's economy. Deep snow often shuts down logging operations for weeks at a time. Heavy rains, so prevalent on the west slope of the Cascades, often have washed out logging operations, making it necessary to rebuild roads, culverts, bridges and railroads before logging can resume.

During the dry summer season, the danger of forest fire is also a part of the life of a logger. In the days of railroad logging it was multiplied by the danger of sparks from steam equipment and from the grind of metal wheels on metal rails as the logging trains moved out of the mountains. In fact, during fire season, men on a speeder followed the loaded trains down the steep grades, dousing and stamping out sparks thrown from the rails. Fire in the forests and in a community surrounded by forests has always been frightening and is sometimes disastrous. Some of the major fires in the woods during the time of big timber operations were reported in *The Arlington Times*.

A fire in August 1917 started in the Danneher Camp and

burned out of control for a week, burning through logged-off areas, scorching standing timber, moving into Sound Timber holdings and burning fiercely on a logged-off tract of land adjoining the town, raising fears for the safety of the community.

In September 1925 sparks from an overheated brake shoe on a logging train started a major fire that swept up North Mountain, heavily damaging Andron's railroad equipment, seven or eight bridges, culverts and two donkey engines.

The late summer and fall of 1929 were extremely dry in the Northwest, and for two weeks fires burned out of control in several areas in the Darrington vicinity. A thick haze of smoke covered the valley, making the hot sun a blurred orange ball in the sky and increasing the problems of new fire spotting for the Forest Service lookouts.

It was during that summer of fire danger that *The Arlington Times* first recorded the practice of "hoot owling" — working in the cooler and more humid hours of 2 a.m. to noon. Some of the camps resorted to the hoot owl shift in an effort to stay open, but some camps closed down completely until the rains resumed in the fall.

Again in the summer of 1930 the same curse of fire struck the mountains, some of the fires man-caused in the logging units and some caused by lightning. Only a drenching rain during the second week of September squelched the fires and cleared the pall of smoke that had settled into the valley for several weeks.

The logger not only contended with nature's problems. Railroad logging operations such as the ones located in the Darrington area were also deeply affected by the strategies of the railroads. A lack of cars to service the Northwest timber industry often caused logging companies to shut down for several weeks at a time until more cars could be located. In 1925 an increase in the railroad freight tariff almost strangled the burgeoning industry. Companies that ran their own private rail lines all the way to tidewater were in an advantageous position. But Sound and Sauk and Andron depended on the Northern Pacific. It was several months before the rate issue was settled and the logging trains began to run again in the Darrington area.

Along with being unpredictable, the logger's life was a dangerous one as well. Injuries were serious and frequent during the railroad logging era, and death was met regularly in the woods. Loggers' wives remember the terror they felt when they heard the logging train pull into the depot blowing seven blasts on its whistle. The signal meant there had been a death in the woods and that the man's body was being brought home. The women would run to the depot to find out who it was, not really wanting to go, but knowing they had to.

Sometimes death and injury were met on the logging trains themselves. One of the most spectacular accidents in Darrington's history occurred in August 1922 when a Mulligan car — a flat car equipped with seats along the sides — jammed against a piece of wood that fell from it and was lifted off the track and dumped bottom side up in a ravine twenty or twenty-five feet below the trestle over which it was passing. Twenty-three men who had been on their way to work for Washington Spar were pinned beneath the derailed car. James B. Woods was killed instantly. Elmer Kaah, Alex Kaah and Stanley McFadden were injured critically. Fifteen others suffered more or less severe injuries.

The injured were placed on another railroad car and taken to the Darrington depot, a distance of about two miles. In the meantime the local telephone operator notified the townspeople that cars and trucks were needed for transportation from the depot to Dr. Blake's hospital and that mattresses were also needed to accommodate the accident victims at the already full hospital. Within minutes mattresses appeared on nearly every porch in town, and a truck made the rounds to pick them up. Cars and trucks lined up at the depot to transfer the injured to the hospital.

Perhaps because of the closeness of death and injury that surrounds them all the time, Darrington people have always been responsive to the griefs and losses of their neighbors. Old grudges and disputes are forgotten as families share in caring for the injured and the grieving. It is part of the strange mixture of toughness and gentleness that the logging life seems to produce. Even in the "safer" times of the 1960's and '70's this compassionate trait was still in evidence, a piece of the town's heritage.

Chapter 12

The Depression

It wasn't enough that railroad car shortages, high rail tariffs, forest fires and deep snows should make consistent logging impossible. Inevitably the Great Depression also made its impact on the logging industry and on Darrington, which by 1929 was almost exclusively a logging town.[1]

A two-month suspension of logging in mid-summer 1929 heralded the difficult times ahead, but most people considered the interruption just one of those caused by a usual fluctuation in the always varying log market. When logging operations resumed on September 4, log traffic on the Northern Pacific Branch quickly rose to normal volume, or about 115 cars a day. Sound and Sauk's shipments were augmented by pole-cutting operations in the Darrington area. Three outfits were cutting and shipping 120-foot poles to help fill part of an order for 15,000 carloads of pilings for the new Ford Motor Co. plant at Edgewater, N.J. The economy couldn't be in too bad a shape.

The summer of 1930, the story was about the same. This time a camp closure ran from July 1 through September; but Sauk planned to resume logging on October 1, and had a crew of 40 men burning slash in preparation for reopening.

October 1 arrived, but Sauk camp didn't open. Neither did Sound nor the Sultan nor Lamson camps down the Branch. *The Arlington Times* headlines on October 2 read: "Logging off until 1931. Operators rescind orders to resume and camps seem to be down for remainder of year. Drop in prices responsible for continued suspension." There seemed to be no hope that logging would resume before the spring of 1931.

Then two weeks later a sudden fluctuation in prices sent some of the logging crews back to the woods for an eight-week respite from unemployment. When that brief flurry of activity was over, though, the Depression had settled firmly into the valley. For two and a half years there would be virtually no employment in the woods. Intermittently during the Depression small logging outfits would operate briefly, taking out poles or cordwood as the market demanded; but work was not consistent. In April 1931 the Darrington columnist for the Arlington paper noted that many of the Darrington men had gone elsewhere in the almost hopeless task of looking for employment. Many had waited through the winter expecting and hoping for Sauk and Sound to reopen in April, but hope died with the springtime.

In September 1932 Sauk put a crew of one hundred men back to work salvaging bucked-up timber that had lain on the ground for two years. Northern Pacific rail crews were alerted to prepare flat cars that had sat on sidings during the long shutdown. Continuation of operations would depend on the still-uncertain log market, but for a time there was some work, and the most welcome sound in Darrington was the sound of the speeder leaving town each morning with a crew of the home guards heading for the woods. A winter layoff that winter of 1932-1933 was followed by a cautious resumption of logging by Sauk and Sound towards spring. The initial shipment of thirty carloads of logs in March 1933 marked the end of the longest shutdown of logging operations in Puget Sound history.

At the outset of the extended layoff in the woods around Darrington some men found work building a road from Darrington to Clear Creek. This was a government work project supervised by the Forest Service and the county. For a few months in 1931 it provided much-needed work and income for heads of families in the Darrington area.

In 1933 a Civilian Conservation Corps camp was established at Darrington, west of the Forest Service ranger station. At its height, the camp housed 200 men. The camp was run by the Army. Work projects were supervised by a U.S. Forest Service foreman. Among the projects the CCC's did in the Darrington area were: 1. Building a truck road up the Sauk that would later become part of the Mountain Loop Highway from Darrington to Verlot; 2. Building a truck road to the Texas Pond ranger station and beyond, along the ridge between the Sauk River and the headwaters of the Stillaguamish; 3. Maintaining and extending a road up the Suiattle River.

According to Harold Engles, district ranger during the CCC period, the men did a lot of valuable work in the district. In addition to road and trail building and maintenance they were also called on for fire control. Engles said that the Forest Service and the Army disagreed on where the men should be billeted. The Forest Service wanted side camps established away from town so that the men would be closer to their jobs and time would not be wasted transporting them back and forth from the main camp. But the Army wanted to keep the men together in one place — and it did.

Officers of the camp in the summer of 1933 were First Lt. Floyd R. Brisack; Second Lt. Charles Adams; Master Sgt. Eastman; Corporal Barguilski, in charge of supply; Pfc. Allen, cook; J.A. Healey, superintendent of field work; Dr. McDaniels, Navy doctor in charge of medical work at Darrington and other camps.

Pay for work in the CCC camp was $30 a month plus food and clothing. Most of the workers were single men between the ages of 18 and 25. Local Experienced Men (LEM), who were older and experienced in forest work, were hired at $35 a month. In June 1933, CCC members on duty at the camp were from Everett, Bellingham, Anacortes, Arlington and Mount Vernon. The CCC camp continued to operate at Darrington until July 1942.

In reading through *The Arlington Times* reports from Darrington during the early years of the Depression, it seems as if nature as well as the economy wanted to play havoc with the people in the mountain community. During the summer of 1931 there was an outbreak of scarlet fever followed by numerous cases of smallpox. Public gatherings were forbidden as county health officers and the local doctors sought to bring the diseases under control.

Heavy snow in the mountains during the winter of 1931-32 was followed by a quick thaw and heavy rains in March 1932. The rampaging Sauk River took out a new railroad bridge built by Sound Timber Co. and a new Skagit County highway bridge at Bennettville. The normally quiet Dan's Creek out towards the Sauk Prairie changed course and washed out new bridge approaches and formed a lake at its mouth. (That summer the temporary lake provided good swimming.) With good luck and lots of dynamite to keep logs from jamming against it, Darrington men saved the new steel bridge across the Sauk at Darrington. Bridges and culverts along the Arlington-Darrington Road were also washed out. For several days after the flood Darrington was isolated with no phones, no roads, no electric power and only one bridge.

The spring continued to be a wet, cold one, but local gardeners began putting in early potatoes and peas as one way to keep ahead of Depression shortages. In mid-May a late freeze wiped out the early gardens and budding fruit trees. The next summer a frost one-inch thick settled over the valley on June 8, wiping out early gardens for the second year in a row.

In May 1935 a small group of local citizens tried a new way to beat the effects of the Depression. The Darrington Pioneers' Exchange,[2] a non-profit cooperative association, was formed in order to provide members with employment and the necessities for living. The small cooperative planned to deal in lumber products. It was closely associated with the Washington State Department of Welfare, Division of Special Programs. First officers were A.E. Burdick, president and general manager; Jeff West, vice president; and Alice Elinor Lambert, secretary-treasurer. Fourteen members were listed in the group's application for funds.

The Exchange originally cut and marketed firewood in order to try to get some ready cash, but its ultimate aim was to build and operate a sawmill, doing its own logging to provide logs for the mill. It negotiated for land from Sam Strom, receiving a warranty deed for some of his mineral claims on Gold Hill and a quit claim deed for some unsurveyed river bar land which would be suitable for a mill location. It then sought to find logging equipment and saw mill equipment, much of which it salvaged from junk yards, bought second hand or got on loan from the State Department of Social Welfare.

Despite many disappointments, disagreements among members, a shortage of money and inadequate equipment, the co-op members built the mill and had it operating by the spring of 1937 — but not as a "successful" venture. The first carload of lumber was rejected by a customer for failing to meet its specifications. The mill operation employed ten men. Altogether the co-op employed thirty-three people in the spring of 1937.

Shortly after its founding in the summer of 1935, the Exchange acquired four lots on the end of Montague Avenue on which to locate its headquarters. It began looking into acquiring sixteen more lots in the same area on which to build housing for members. One of the co-op's aims was to build a home for any member in need of one. Sometimes the need for housing was crucial. At one meeting a member announced that his wife had served notice that if the co-op didn't build them a house she was going to leave him. The co-op board apparently took the threat seriously, agreeing to build a cabin the Sunday after next. Only green lumber was available, but they'd build it out of that so the family would have a house. The co-op could not afford to buy flooring so the board agreed to build a double floor of green lumber and cover it over with an old rug until its treasury was built up. The Exchange secretary offered to give the family a window out of her office at headquarters so that the cabin would have four windows. And so the house was built.

The Pioneers' Exchange was plagued by difficulties. Hard-working members complained about people who did not do their share of the work, and shirkers were put out, if necessary, by a vote of the membership. Leaders of various ventures — commissary manager, blacksmith shop foreman, mill foreman, woods foreman — were installed and fired from their jobs often in a matter of weeks or months by the strong general manager, A.E. Burdick, or by a vote of the membership. At one point Burdick called for his own brother's resignation as woods foreman because production was lagging and the group had to produce to survive. The brother refused to resign and was fired.

Heading the commissary was apparently a particularly difficult and thankless job as one woman after another tried to handle the grocery purchasing and distribution to the co-op members.

For a long period as the co-op got underway, time was the medium of exchange since there was no way as yet to make money. Members presented their cash needs at board meetings. The cooperative paid what it could from its meager treasury to meet these needs, but there was never enough to go around. One member presented a bill for $68 including $5 for lights, $4 for groceries, $9 for a sewing machine, $15 for shoes and clothes for his family, $5 in back rent and $30 for medical attention for his pregnant wife. The co-op gave him $25 to spread out over his needs as best he could.

In spite of all its difficulties, including community suspicion, the Darrington Pioneers' Exchange did provide work and a means of sustenance for a few families during some of the bleakest years of the Depression, but it never entirely succeeded and it died as better times returned to the valley.

Perhaps a measure of the effect of the Depression on Darrington lies in the fact that in 1932 the town's eleven street lights were turned off for lack of funds. In many ways gloom had descended on the town.

However the Depression had its bright side. Not able to work, the people spent their energy and time in community activities. Boxing, which had begun to be popular during the 1920's took on more importance as boxers from Tacoma, Bellingham, Arlington, Everett and Darrington met regularly in bouts at old King Tut Hall. A basketball first touched the community boards during the Depression, and both men's and women's community teams saw action against high school counterparts in Darrington and in other towns. In the first contests, held at Firemen's Hall, the firemen defeated the high school boys 38-16, and the women's team beat the high school girls 40-11.

The Women's Home Demonstration Club, Methodist and Baptist Ladies' Aid Societies and the Baptist choir all saw increased participation during the Depression years. The Baptist choir participated in quarterly "singing conventions" in the tradition of the South. As many as 225 people from Darrington and other communities attended an all-day singing convention in Darrington in the spring of 1931. The Sauguamish Club, which held dances twice monthly, boasted 100 members in 1932.

It was during the Depression that Darrington sought a name for itself as a ski place. Local skiers under the leadership of Nels Bruseth built a ski and toboggan run on Brumby Hill in 1932. That ski run ran east from the gravel pit along what is now Alvord Street. Others who initiated the winter sports activities were Paul Woodward, Joe Keenan and Harold Engles.

When Brumby Hill proved unsatisfactory, the Darrington Winter Sports Club, aided by the CCC's, began developing Ski Hill, an area south of town now owned by the county but then owned by the Forest Service. A ski jump tower designed by Bruseth and sled and toboggan runs were built there. Slushy weather often doomed plans for competitive ski events. Nonetheless, the Darrington ski slopes and cross country ski runs drew both local and out-of-town winter sports enthusiasts for several years, and maps still note a winter sports area adjacent to Darrington though it has long been abandoned.

Chapter 13

The Trucks Begin
To Roll

As long as there has been logging there have been "gyppos" — independent loggers working alone to cut, haul and sell timber on their own. In the Darrington area some gyppos got their start in the Depression, logging small patches of timber in an effort to keep busy and to make a little money while the big railroad logging outfits sat out bad times. Trucks — a motley fleet of them at best — provided the wheels for the small logging ventures and heralded a new era in logging methods. After the Depression many loggers who went back to work for the big companies found it profitable to do small logging jobs on their own on the weekends. They used a minimum of equipment and a great deal of ingenuity as they loaded, hauled and sold logs that Sauk and Sound had cut and rejected.

Some of the earliest truck gyppos in the area were Kuntz and Wright, later to be known as Wright and Sons, who began truck logging in 1932 and sold to Al Greenleaf in 1946. (Greenleaf's trucks were always readily identifiable through the rear-view of one's car as they bore down on a too-slow driver. Attached to the radiators was a "green leaf" insignia.) Usitalo Brothers came in

1939 and sold to Roy Loughnan in 1943 who sold out to Jones and Anderson in 1959. An incomplete list of gyppos who have worked in the Darrington area would include Glen Rankin, Sam Forrister, Jack Faucett, Dave Buchanan, Bryson Brothers, Brick West, Al McMahan, Galbraith Brothers, Clayton Reece, Wright and Sons, Roy Loughnan and RK Inc. Many of these started out with one man working completely alone — true gyppos — but some grew into bigger outfits, employing anywhere from five to thirty men. Some loggers consider the largest of these outfits a little too big to still fit the "gyppo" category.

Truck logging was very different from railroad logging. As truck logging began in the 1930's and 40's it was financially within the reach of many independently minded loggers who preferred to work for themselves rather than for a corporate employer like Sauk River Lumber Co. or Sound Timber. There was a versatility and mobility in truck logging that railroad logging did not provide. Trucks could go where trains could not. Toward the end of Sauk's stay in the Darrington area, the company used trucks to haul logs from the woods to a reload area where the logs were put on railroad cars to be shipped out of town, thus combining the two means of transportation for the best efficiency.

The small logging outfits that began in the 30's and 40's and which flourished in the 50's and 60's were called gyppos because they operated on financial shoestrings compared to the large logging camps and cut corners or gypped on crew makeup to save money. Gyppos did their own financing, bought timber sales independently, ran their own operations, and sold logs wherever they wanted to. They bid on sales that were too small for the railroad outfits to profitably log. After the railroads pulled out, the gyppos were the salvage crews of the woods, often re-logging areas where the big outfits had left "inferior" timber standing or on the ground. Sometimes gyppos cleaned out big log jams that clogged the rivers, selling the salvaged logs to mills down below. There was a lot of clean up, for railroad logging was wasteful. The companies wanted only the big timber that was absolutely at its prime. A log with a streak of blue in one part of it, indicating it was beginning to rot, would be left as junk. Trees two or three feet through were considered too small to bother with. Fir was in demand. Cedar and hemlock were considered inferior. So there was unbelievable waste. In the 1950's and 60's, as the awareness grew that resources need to be conserved, the junk, the rejects from the railroad logging era became valuable. Blue-streaked logs that had been lying on the ground for fifteen or twenty years could be salvaged. The rotted ends could be cut off and the sound center portions cut for lumber. The salvage work kept the gyppos busy for many years. Sometimes loggers salvaged fallen and bucked logs lying beneath a canopy of forty- or fifty-foot tall trees, two and three feet through, the second growth on a rail-road-logged site. As the clean up work ended, the gyppos began to bid on new timber. Often it was second growth that had flourished after the railroad loggers made the virgin cuts.

As gyppos developed, they often worked under contract to large companies such as Scott, Georgia-Pacific, Weyerhauser and mills like Everett Plywood, Busey and Darrington's Summit Timber Mill. In a contract setup, the large company pays for the timber sale and makes a contract with the gyppo to pay the logger so much per thousand board feet of timber cut. Often the big company pays the gyppo an advance in order to get the logging underway. The gyppo handles the payroll for his men and supplies all the equipment for the job.

Life as a gyppo logger is not easy. Hours are long. When you are working for yourself, one gyppo said, you don't quit at quitting time; you keep working until all the work you planned to do is done. Sometimes it's a twelve or sixteen-hour day. You come home bone weary. It seems you never come home in time for supper. (Ask a logger's wife.) But you'd rather be working on your own than for some "big outfit." Walt Robinson Sr.[1] claims that gyppos work more efficiently and take better care of their equipment than men working for a big corporation. They know that the cost of lost or broken equipment will directly affect the size of their profit when the job is done. Robinson explained it this way: "I'm working out there in the woods and I've got a $20 choker. When night comes I'm going to remember where that choker is. I won't go home and forget about it and say, 'Oh, well, the company will buy me a new one tomorrow.' "

Gyppoing has its ups and downs. Sometimes you clear a pro-fit. Sometimes you lose. It's an uncertain way to make a living. Why, then, have so many men stuck to gyppoing so long? "It's about like taking dope, I guess," Robinson said. "It gets a hold of you and you can't get free." The challenge and risks have their appeal to an independent breed of men. When you are a gyppo, you improvise, you make equipment work that others say can't work, and when you get the job done, you really know you've accomplished something.

Many gyppos started out with only one piece of equipment. Walt Robinson Sr., for instance, started out with one "cat" with which to clear land. Later, working alone or picking up a partner as needed, he began salvage work and began expanding his inventory of equipment. In the 1960's he and his son, Walt Jr., and Don Knowles incorporated the average-size outfit they had put together. When RK Inc., as it was called, was sold out to G & D Logging in 1970 it employed twelve to fifteen men and operated four log trucks, one yarder-tower outfit, two caterpillars, three old shovels and an assortment of old pickups and gravel trucks.

According to Robinson, the height of gyppoing was in the 1960's when the export market opened up and left the gyppos free to sell directly for export. When the restraints were put on log exporting again, the gyppos went back to contract logging and were dependent once again on the mills. By 1970 many of the gyppos in the Darrington area were finding it hard to continue to operate either independently or as contract loggers. Several gyppos sold out at that time to the newly formed G & D Logging Co. which provides logs for the Summit Timber Mill. With the exception of a few holdouts, it looked as if the economics of logging had put an end to the independent logger's heyday.

Unless a man is already in logging or inherits a logging outfit, the seventies are no time to try to make a start in gyppoing, Robinson said. A man trying to start out as a gyppo now would have to make an initial outlay of about $500,000. "If you have that kind of money, you're foolish to risk it in the logging business. It doesn't make sense," he said. Robinson put out $2,800 in 1947 to get a start, and more than a thousand of that was borrowed. Today one piece of logging equipment may cost $300,000 to $400,000. "You have to move a lot of timber to pay for that," he commented. There may be other parts of the country — Alaska, for instance — where such an enterprise might still work, but those days in the Darrington area are past.

Brick West began gyppoing in 1951 after he left his job at Georgia-Pacific. He logged alone or with his son for twenty years, retiring in 1971. He started out with a gravel truck and a flat bed truck. A cherry picker on the front of the gravel truck loaded the logs onto the flatbed. His first job was salvaging logs along Scott Paper Company's right of ways.

Though West "officially" began gyppoing in 1951, he was familiar with it before that. In 1939 when he was head loader on

Sauk's reload, he and his friend Merlin "Tug" Thomas loaded up rejected logs on the weekend and sold them to Robinson Plywood in Everett, hauling them in Tug's old truck. Sauk had given West permission to salvage the logs, assuming that he wanted them for firewood. When Sauk found out he and his friend were making a profit off the company's rejects, Brick and "Tug" were ordered to stop. The big logs, often with just a "blue streak" in them, were left to rot.

Brick and Tug were not completely stymied. They found other logs in other places that no one wanted, and working on weekends they made more than they made all week at their regular logging jobs.

As Sauk River Lumber Co. prepared to leave the valley in the 1950's the tempo of truck logging increased. By 1959 — about five or six years after Sauk left — a hundred logging trucks operated by a large number of gyppos were hauling into or through Darrington everyday. Some of the gyppo operations remained small like Brick West's family outfit. However, some of the early gyppos grew to the point that they could hardly be considered gyppos any longer. One such outfit was Jones and Anderson, which, with considerable corporate and partnership changes, is part of Summit Timber Co., Darrington's largest employer today. [2]

In 1935 Ivan and Robert Jones were truck logging with a small crew in Whatcom Co. In 1938 the brothers formed a partnership with Carl and Rudolph Anderson. In the spring of 1942 Jones and Anderson moved up to Texas Pond near Darrington to log some privately owned timber there. The crew of about twenty who came with the outift planned to stay for about six months. However, when that logging project was completed, the partnership began to bid on Forest Service sales, and Jones and Anderson was in Darrington to stay.

In 1945 a corporation of the stockholders of Jones and Anderson, E.E. Boyd, Norman Levine and R.A. Boyd began to build a shingle mill. They called it Three Rivers Mill Co. In 1948 the operation grew by the addition of Conifer Timber Co, headed by Burke G. Barker. A plywood plant was built and the company became Three Rivers Plywood and Timber Co. Jones and Anderson were the loggers for all the mills.

Jones and Anderson and the other stockholders sold out to Summit Timber Co. in 1959. At that time Summit was operating the Fortson Mill a few miles down the road. In 1959-60 the mill equipment from Fortson was moved to Darrington where the mill has grown and changed with the times. In 1974 the mill alone employed about 300 persons.

Jones and Anderson continued logging for the mill until about 1964-65. Then for five or six years the mill depended entirely on contract loggers — both large and small gyppo outfits — to keep it supplied with timber. In 1970 an entirely new group of stockholders formed the G & D Logging Co., buying out and absorbing many of the gyppo loggers in the area. G & D is now the major logging outfit for the Summit Mill.

During the almost three decades of its work, Jones and Anderson logged two billion board feet of timber, including 100-foot logs which were especially milled in Anacortes during World War II to provide keels for wooden mine sweepers. In the decade of 1964-1974, one billion board feet of logs were cut at the Summit Mill.

When the railroad logging companies withdrew from the valley, it was the end of a colorful era. The big, impressive steam machinery and the huge steam locomotives were gone. As the railroads left, many loggers abandoned the valley, too. There was no longer a large, self-contained logging camp housing over a hundred men, or, as in the case of Sound and Danneher camps, families as well. Loggers who remained were the "home guards," the men who had put down family roots in town and on the scattered farms on the town's outskirts. The rumble of the big locys punctuated by the special wail of the steam whistle was replaced by the drone of logging trucks and the irritating percussion of "jake brakes." Another era had begun.

Darrington, well established as a logging town, bridged the gap between the era of railroads and the era of trucks with its usual spunk. With pride in their past logging exploits in an era that soon would become legendary, the logging men set their sights on the future of the logging industry. They penetrated deeper and deeper into the mountains, building roads to reach the timber high up on precipitous slopes. They adapted and changed their logging methods, harnessing them to new technology. Not far off in the future was the era of the helicopter and of aerial logging. When the time came, these Darrington loggers would adapt to that too. It's part of their heritage, it's part of the way their town has survived — mining the "green gold" of the forests, making a life for themselves in what was all wilderness not so long ago.

NOTES

CHAPTER 2   THE PLACE AND ITS NATIVE PEOPLE

[1] Contained in Nels Bruseth's papers, University of Washington, Seattle. Copies of the papers were shared with me by his widow, Beate Staff Falke Bruseth, in 1969.

[2] Nels Bruseth, *Indian Stories and Legends of the Stillaguamish and Allied Tribes*, 1926, p. 12.

[3] *Ibid.*, p.p. 7, 8.

[4] Information for this section was taken from the Opinion and Findings in Fact presented before the Indian Claims Commission, The Upper Skagit Tribe of Indians, petitioner, v. the United States of America, defendant, Docket 92, decided March 25, 1960. Much of the Opinion and Findings in Fact was based on testimony by Dr. June McCormick Collins, whose book, *Valley of the Spirits: The Upper Skagit Indians of Western Washington* (University of Washington, 1974), presents a full and far more expert account of this group of Indians.

[5] I am grateful to Miss Edith Bedal, Darrington, for her interviews and for her sharing notes and materials from her private collection. I interviewed her on November 24, 1972, and on December 13 and 20, 1972. Her sister, Mrs. Jean Bedal Fox, was also present on November 24, 1972.

[6] A copy of William Moses' statement is in the private collection of Miss Bedal.

[7] Information taken from an undated and unidentified news clipping in the private collection of Miss Bedal.

[8] Information on the *speequods* was taken from an unpublished article written in the 1930's or 40's by Alice Elinor Lambert, a Darrington writer, and was substantiated by Miss Bedal.

[9] Spellings of Indian words in this section are from Miss Lambert's notes. Nels Bruseth used spellings very close to these in his writings. Linguists would provide more accurate renderings of the Indian sounds.

[10] James Mooney, "The Ghost Dance Religion: The Shakers of Puget Sound." Extract from *The Fourteenth Annual Report of the Bureau of American Ethnology,* 1896. Facsimile reproduction by The Shorey Book Store, Seattle, 1966, p. 750.

[11] *Ibid.*

[12] *Ibid.,* p. 755

CHAPTER 3   EXPLORERS AND PROSPECTORS

[1] Information regarding Linsley's exploration is taken from "Pioneering in the Cascade Country," *Civil Engineering* Vol. 2, No. 6 (June 1932): p.p. 339-344.

[2] *Ibid.,* p. 344

[3] Sam Strom, ' 'Reminiscences, 1893-1934," microfilm, University of Washington. The original is in the private collection of Alice Elinor Lambert for whose benefit it was written in 1936.

[4] *History of Skagit and Snohomish Counties, Washington, Their People, Their Commerce and Their Resources with an Outline of the Early History of the State of Washington.* (Chicago: Interstate Publishing Co., 1906), p. 404ff.

[5] *Ibid.*

[6] *Ibid.*

[7] *Arlington Times,* June 7, 1902. (Issues from April 6, 1895 through March 28, 1973 are on microfilm at the University of Washington Library and were used extensively in research.)

[8] *Ibid.,* May 5, 1897.

[9] The story of Jesse Benson Price has been pieced together from notes and articles appearing in the *Arlington Times* from 1903 to 1908.

[10] Lawrence "Toby" Freese was interviewed May 21, 1970, July 6, 1970, May 3, 1973 and May 17, 1973 and provided much information for this book.

CHAPTER 4   EARLY MILLS

[1] *Arlington Times,* May 4, 1907.

[2] *Ibid.,* June 18, 1910.

[3] *Ibid.,* June 4, 1910.

[4] *Ibid.,* October 24, 1914.

[5] *Ibid.,* October 31, 1914.

CHAPTER 5   THE SETTLERS

[1] Much of the information in this chapter is from Nels Bruseth's papers.

[2] Flora McCulloch Howe was interviewed at her home in Darrington October 25 and 29, 1968, December 1968 and February 1973.

[3] The information on Fred Fuller was compiled from short notes appearing in the *Arlington Times* from 1897 on, from an undated and unidentified news clipping in the possession of Harold Engles, and from personal recollections of Harold Engles, Lawrence "Toby" Freese, Flora McCulloch Howe and Paul Woodward.

CHAPTER 6   SCHOOL BELLS IN THE VALLEY

[1] Information on the early schools is from Nels Bruseth's papers.

[2] Information about Newton Castle Rhoads was supplied by his daughter, Mrs. Earl L. Zylstra of Tacoma, Washington, and by Lawrence "Toby" Freese, Pearl Towne Reece and Flora Howe.

[3] Pearl Towne Reece was interviewed in her home near Sauk Prairie in the spring of 1970.

[4] Information in the rest of this chapter is taken from minutes of the Darrington School Board, January 1924 through January 1936. The minutes were located in the office of Darrington Elementary School. Minutes prior to 1924 and minutes from 1936 through the 1950's could not be located for research.

CHAPTER 7   RELIGION COMES TO TOWN

[1] Information on the Methodist Church is taken from a history of the church compiled by Flora Howe in 1966 to commemorate the church's fifieth anniversary.

[2] Roy M. Owen was interviewed March 7, 1973, at his home in Mount Vernon, Washington.

[3] Much of the information on First Baptist Church is quoted verbatim from "A History of First Baptist Church of Darrington," compiled by the author in commemoration of the church's fiftieth anniversary in July 1971. A copy of the history is in the church records.

[4] First Baptist Church record book, Vol. 1, p. 52.

[5] Information on the Roman Catholic Church in the Darrington vicinity was supplied by the Rev. Edward C. Boyle, formerly a priest in Darrington and now a priest in Renton, Washington.

[6] Information on the Pentecostal Churches was provided by Mrs. Fred Rensink, Mrs. C.B. Andrews and the Rev. Robert Fox, former pastor of Glad Tidings Assembly of God Church.

[7] Information on Mountain View Baptist Church was supplied by Mrs. Glendon Moore.

[8] Information about the Episcopal Church in Darrington was supplied by the Rev. Walter W. McNeil Jr., Archdeacon of Olympia.

CHAPTER 8   DOING BUSINESS

[1] *Arlington Times,* July 24, 1897.

[2] *Ibid.,* August 1914.

[3] *Ibid.,* Sept. 2, 1915.

[4] *Ibid.*, July 15, 1915.

[5] *Everett Herald*, December 12, 1966.

[6] W. Ward Woodward was interviewed October 30, 1968, January 1969 and March 8, 1973. He provided much information on early events and many of the photographs which appear in this book.

[7] *Arlington Times*, July 30, 1910.

[8] Margaret Bundy Callahan, "The Last Frontier," *The Cascades*, Roderick Peattie, ed. (The Vanguard Press, N.Y., 1949), pp. 52-53.

[9] Roy F. Wolfe was interviewed February 28, 1973, at his home in Marysville, Washington.

[10] Information from "Darrington — This Is Your Life," a script written by Ida Loughnan for the 1959 Timber Bowl celebration.

[11] *Arlington Times*, December 8, 1900.

[12] *Ibid.*, March 30, 1901.

[13] *Ibid.*, February 13, 1904.

[14] *Everett Herald*, December 12, 1966.

[15] *Arlington Times*, January 11, 1923.

[16] *Ibid.*, November 22, 1923.

[17] *Ibid.*, February 1, 1924.

[18] Throughout the book reference is made to Harold Engles, U.S. Forest Service Ranger in Darrington from 1927 to 1937 and from 1943 to 1958. Now retired and living on a farm near Whitehorse, he and his wife, Anna May, were of invaluable help to me throughout all my research.

[19] *Arlington Times*, July 9, 1925.

[20] Loughnan, "Darrington — This Is Your Life."

[21] *Ibid.*

[22] Quoted in *Arlington Times*, April 3, 1915.

[23] Quoted in *Arlington Times*, April 17, 1915.

[24] Frank Lock, now a resident of Tacoma, Washington, was interviewed by telephone January 25, 1975.

[25] Information was obtained by letter from Cliff Danielson, now owner of the *Stanwood* (Washington) *News*, January 10, 1975.

[26] Information was obtained by letter from Allison R. "Ace" Comstock, now onwer of *Port Orchard* (Washington) *Independent*, October 1974.

CHAPTER 9   THE TARHEELS

[1] For a very complete look at the Southern Appalachian settler in the Northwest, see Woodrow Rexford Clevinger, *The Southern Appalachian Highlanders in Western Washington* (Seattle, University of Washington, M.A. Thesis, geography, 1940) and Clevinger, *The Western Washington Cascades: A Study of Migration*

and Mountain Settlement (Seattle, University ot Washington, Ph.D. Thesis, geography, 1955). Both are in the University of Washington Library.

[2] I have been told two origins of the name "Tarheel." One is that North Carolinians are so loyal to their state and so prone to stay put there that it is as if they had "tar on their heels." Another version is that people from that state move as slowly as if they had "tar on their heels." There are probably a dozen more folk explanations for the term. Some North Carolinians I've met consider the term derogatory and don't want to be called a "Tarheel." Others take pride in it as a symbol of the home country which they preserve in custom and accent even after several generations in the Northwest.

[3] Octavia Bryson was interviewed in her home in Darrington May 20, 1970, three days after her eightieth birthday. She died November 14, 1972.

[4] Alta Long was interviewed at her home near Sauk Prairie November 22 and 30, 1972. Her sister, Nel Adams, also participated in the second interview.

[5] Pearl Lewis was interviewed at the home of her son, Robert, near Sauk Prairie, September 24, 1974. She died in July 1975.

[6] Minnie Cabe was interviewed in her home in Darrington, June 26, 1974.

CHAPTER 10   SMALL-TOWN MEDICINE

[1] Information on Dr. Blake was compiled from interviews with the late Dr. N.C. Riddle, W. Ward Woodward, Pearl Wilson Hasenyager, Blake's former nurse; Mrs. Mary Cameron and Mrs. Bessie Sather, Dr. Blake's daughters; and from a scrapbook made by Mrs. Marguerite Spaulding, chairman of the committee which sent Blake to the World Series. The scrapbook is in Mrs. Sather's private collection.

[2] Information on Dr. Riddle was compiled from interviews with him in September 1969, from an interview with his nurse, Mrs. Pearl Wilson Hasenyager, May 16, 1973; and from correspondence in July 1974 with Ellen Olson Pollard, his former nurse, now a resident of Lake Stevens, Washington.

CHAPTER 11   BIG TIMBER

[1] *Arlington Times,* March 27, 1897.

[2] Frances Moll Soper was interviewed at her home in Arlington, Washington, April 19, 1973.

[3] Information in the section that follows was taken from *Historical Data — Mt. Baker National Forest. A Handbook of Historical Facts and Figures* compiled by Newton Fields, approved by H. Phil Bradner, forest supervisor, 1950. A copy of the report is located at the Darrington Ranger Station.

[4] A copy of the contract is located in the historical file, Darrington District Ranger Station.

[5] For this entire chapter on logging I relied heavily on the *Arlington Times* for dated material as well as on information supplied by the men mentioned in the text.

[6] Tom Tathum was interviewed in Darrington, June 27, 1974.

[7] Information on Dave Mallonee was provided by Mrs. Hilda Mallonee Bryson, his daughter, interviewed November 29, 1972; Burke Henson; and Don Davis of the *Everett Herald*.

[8] Burke Henson was interviewed at his home in Darrington on May 23, 1973.

[9] Fallers felled the trees; buckers cut them up into lengths suitable for loading; scalers measured the logs to determine the amount of timber in each.

[10] J.T. "Tom" Ashe was interviewed at his home in Darrington on May 23, 1973.

[11] Lawrence "Brick" West was interviewed at his home in Darrington on December 28, 1973, January 3, 1973 and March 5, 1975.

CHAPTER 12   THE DEPRESSION

[1] Details of the Depression's affect on Darrington have been compiled from almost weekly articles and correspondent's notes appearing in the *Arlington Times* during those years.

[2] Minutes of Darrington Pioneers' Exchange, University of Washington Library.

CHAPTER 13   THE TRUCKS BEGIN TO ROLL

[1] Walter Robinson Sr. was interviewed at his home in Swede Heaven near Darrington on March 4, 1975.

[2] Information for this section on Jones and Anderson and Summit Timber was supplied by Robert E. Jones, June 26, 1974.